LAW, AND ETHICS
Business,

DEVELOPING ANALYTICAL AND CRITICAL THINKING SKILLS

Fourth Edition
REVISED PRINTING

Six Focus Areas of Law

CONSTITUTIONAL LAW
CONTRACT LAW
CRIMINAL LAW
EVIDENCE LAW
PROPERTY LAW
TORT LAW

Frederick D. Jones, J.D.
Cristen Dutcher, J.D.
Kennesaw State University

Kendall Hunt
publishing company

publishing company

www.kendallhunt.com
Send all inquiries to:
4050 Westmark Drive
Dubuque, IA 52004-1840

Previously titled Business Law Handbook

Copyright © 2007, 2008, 2010, 2011 by Kendall Hunt Publishing Company

ISBN 978-1-4652-2079-0

Contents

This revision of the fourth edition of *Business, Law, and Ethics: Developing Analytical & Critical Thinking Skills* delivers the same quality information included in the first three editions with several important updates. First, all website and date references have been updated with current information. Second, exercise questions have been rewritten and changed to bring more clarity to those assignments. Finally, the topic area sections of this text have been condensed and clarified for ease of use.

The purpose of this book is first to supplement a legal studies or business law textbook with succinct and clear information on six key areas of the law and ethics in business. This book is to be used as a handbook or reference for quick information, but also a tool for building core critical-thinking and analytical skills in the law and ethics. Important references in this book are the Certified Public Accountants Code of Professional Conduct, the Georgia Rules of Professional Conduct, and the Georgia Code of Judicial Conduct. Even if a student does not choose one of these careers, knowledge of the rules that dictate the ethical requirements for public servants, like CPAs, lawyers, and judges, is imperative. Too often those public servants abuse their positions and act unethically, hurting the public in the process. With extra knowledge of these codes and rules, the public can command proper behavior and activity from those who serve them.

Another major focus is Business Ethics. How many times have we seen a corporation fail because of a lack of integrity and ethical behavior within the leadership? When this happens, it affects the entire community. Often the public does not know what to do, where to go, or who to complain to. We will look at the rules of professional conduct that applies to attorneys, judges, and accountants in the State of Georgia who often stand or sit in judgment of ethical wrongdoers.

After you have carefully worked through this handbook, we hope you will have a better appreciation of what to do or where to go when faced with an ethical conflict. But most importantly, we hope you will be able to avoid the pitfalls of the legally challenged by making quality, legal, and ethical decisions because of your legal reasoning skills.

*T*HIS HANDBOOK IS ORIENTED TOWARD ALL BUSINESS STUDENTS and especially those getting ready to take the CPA and/or BAR examination. The objective is to assist in the understanding and application of law as it pertains to business transactions and accounting practices. The questions are designed to encourage critical thinking and to increase knowledge of business laws.

The key feature of law is critical thinking. The goal is to eliminate the hypothetical and to concentrate solely on fact. When approaching the questions in this study guide, it is important not to assume information that is not given in the question. Look at the key facts in the case, understand where the issues lie, and apply the rule based on the facts.

What Is Legal Reasoning?

Legal Reasoning is the process used by judges in deciding what law applies to a given dispute and then applying that law to the specific facts or circumstances of the case. Through the use of legal reasoning, judges harmonize their decisions with those that have been made before, as the doctrine of *stare decisis* requires.

Students of business law and the legal environment also engage in legal reasoning. For example, one may be asked to provide answers for some of the case problems that appear at the end of every chapter in this text. Each problem describes the facts of a particular dispute and the legal question at issue. If assigned a case problem, one will be asked to determine how a court would answer that question, and why. In other words, one will need to give legal reasons for whatever conclusion one may reach. We look here at the basic steps involved in legal reasoning and then describe some forms of reasoning that are commonly used by the courts in making their decisions.

There Is No One "Right" Answer[1]

Many persons believe that there is one "right" answer to every legal question. In most situations involving a legal controversy, there is no single "right" answer. Good arguments can often be made to support either side of a legal controversy. Quite often, a case does not present the situation of a "good" person suing a "bad" person. In many cases, both parties have acted in good faith in some measure or have acted in bad faith to some degree.

Additionally, each judge has her or his own personal beliefs and philosophy that shape, at least to some extent, the process of legal reasoning. This means that the outcome of a particular lawsuit before a court can never be predicted with absolute certainty. In fact, in some cases, even though the weight of the law would seem to favor one party's position, judges, through creative legal reasoning, have found ways to rule in favor of the other party in the interest of preventing injustice.

∞ Basic Steps in Legal Reasoning: What Is IRAC?

At times, the legal arguments set forth in court opinions are relatively simple and brief. At other times, the arguments are complex and lengthy. Regardless of the length of a legal argument, the basic steps of the legal reasoning process remain the same. These steps, which one can follow when analyzing cases and case problems, form what is commonly referred to as the *IRAC method* of legal reasoning. IRAC is an acronym formed from the first letters of the following words: Issue, Rule, Application, and Conclusion.

IRAC is a method of approaching a legal issue that breaks down the facts of the case and allows for critical examination. IRAC is a simple technique and can be applied to all the questions in this study guide. This process is an effective way to organize thought processes and to guarantee that all parts of the legal analysis are present.

The four-step outline of the IRAC legal reasoning process is as follows:

1. **Issue**—the issue is the main question of fact that is present in the case.
   1. Read the case
   2. Note the questions at hand
   3. Order the issues logically if more than one is present

2. **Rule**—the rule is the application of law to the issue(s) spotted. Approach this step like an algebraic equation and show all parts of the rule applied. The law is a hand, not a finger. Always remember to spell out all the elements of the law (hand) and don't just give one point (finger).
   1. What the rule is
   2. How the courts apply the rule
   3. What the limitations of the rule are

3. **Application**—the process of applying the rule and explaining the thought process in a logical way. Remember, this is not the conclusion.
   1. How the rule should be applied
   2. Understand the reasoning behind the law applied
   3. What other possible applications of law were rejected
   4. Show an examination of the facts

4. **Conclusion**—summary of the application of the rule.
   1. Consider possible remedies
   2. Consider both sides position

To Apply the IRAC Method, You Would Ask the Following Questions:

1. **What are the key facts and issues?** Suppose that a plaintiff comes before the court claiming assault (a wrongful and intentional action in which one person makes another fearful of immediate physical harm—part of a class of actions called *torts*). The plaintiff claims that the defendant threatened her while she was sleeping. Although the plaintiff was unaware that she was being threatened, her roommate heard the defendant make the threat. The legal issue, or question, raised by these facts is whether the defendant's actions constitute the tort of assault, given that the plaintiff was not aware of those actions at the time they occurred.

2. **What rules of law apply to the case?** A rule of law may be a rule stated by the courts in previous decisions, a state or federal statute, or a state or federal administrative agency regulation. In our hypothetical case, the plaintiff **alleges** (claims) that the defendant committed a tort. Therefore, the applicable law is the common law of torts—specifically, tort law governing assault. Case precedents involving similar facts and issues would be relevant. Often, more than one rule of law will be applicable to a case.

3. **How do the rules of law apply to the particular facts and circumstances of this case?** This step is often the most difficult one because each case presents a unique set of facts, circumstances, and parties. Although cases may be similar, no two cases are ever identical in all respects. Normally, judges (and lawyers and law students) try to find **cases on point**—previously decided cases that are as similar as possible to the one under consideration.

4. **What conclusion should be drawn?** This step normally presents few problems. Usually, the conclusion is evident if the previous three steps have been followed carefully.

Helpful Hints

When approaching the topic of law and legal reasoning, there seems to be an overwhelming amount of information that needs to be retained. Law, however, is not a topic that can simply be memorized but one that must be understood and applied as well. Critical thinking skills are crucial in law. Therefore, when discussing an emotional legal topic always remember to stay on the issue and process your thoughts. Below are some legal discussion tips:

- Always start your answer with "generally speaking" and move to the issue.
- Never or rarely answer "yes" or "no".
- Don't be conclusive.
- Be confident—jurors are everyday experts with no special training.
- Leave your emotions outside.
- Do not hate nor fall in love with the parties in the fact pattern.
- Brief the case—find the key points, apply IRAC.
- Understand the rules and reasons—understand why the law is applied.
- Remember the source.
- If possible, read the transcripts yourself.
- Remember the media sells news.
- Remember you are innocent until proven guilty.
- Finally, remember the law is a "hand" and not a "finger"; you must list the elements or rules of law and apply the elements and rules to the fact and come to a conclusion. Rarely if ever will you give a one (finger) word answer such as yes or no.

Constitutional Law Outline: Overview

The terms Constitution, constitutional, and unconstitutional refer to the federal Constitution unless indicated otherwise. Approximately half of the Constitutional Law questions for each Multistate Bar Examination (MBE) will be based on category IV, and approximately half will be based on the remaining categories, I, II, and III.

I. THE NATURE OF JUDICIAL REVIEW

A. Organization and relationship of state and federal courts in a federal system

B. Jurisdiction
1. Constitutional basis
2. Congressional power to define and limit
3. The Eleventh Amendment and state sovereign immunity

C. Judicial review in operation
1. The "case or controversy" requirement including the prohibition on advisory opinions, standing, ripeness, and mootness
2. The "adequate and independent state ground"
3. Political questions and justiciability

II. THE SEPARATION OF POWERS

A. The powers of Congress
1. Commerce, taxing, and spending
2. War, defense, and foreign affairs
3. Power to enforce the Thirteenth, Fourteenth, and Fifteenth Amendments
4. Other powers

B. The powers of the president
1. As chief executive, including the take care clause
2. As commander in chief
3. Treaty and foreign affairs powers
4. Appointment and removal of officials

C. Federal interbranch relationships
  1. Congressional limits on the executive
  2. The Presentment requirement and the president's power to veto or to withhold action
  3. Non-delegation doctrine
  4. Executive, legislative, and judicial immunities

III. THE RELATIONS OF NATION AND STATES IN A FEDERAL SYSTEM
  A. Intergovernmental immunities
    1. Federal immunity from state law
    2. State immunity from federal law, including the Tenth Amendment
  B. Federalism-based limits on state authority
    1. Negative implications of the commerce clause
    2. Supremacy clause and preemption
    3. Full faith and credit
    4. Authorization of otherwise invalid state action

IV. INDIVIDUAL RIGHTS
  A. State action
  B. Due Process
    1. Substantive due process
      a. Fundamental rights
      b. Other rights and interests
    2. Procedural due process, including personal jurisdiction
  C. Equal protection
    1. Fundamental rights
    2. Classifications subject to heightened scrutiny
    3. Rational basis review
  D. Takings
  E. Other protections, including the privileges and immunities clauses, the contracts clause, unconstitutional conditions, bills of attainder, and ex post facto laws
  F. First Amendment freedoms
    1. Freedom of religion and separation of church and state
      a Free exercise
      b. Establishment
    2. Freedom of expression and association
      a. Content-based regulation of content of protected expression
      b. Content-neutral regulation of protected expression
      c. Regulation of unprotected expression
      d. Regulation of commercial speech

      e. Regulation of, or impositions upon, public school students, public employment, licenses, or benefits based upon exercise of expressive or associational rights

      f. Regulation of expressive conduct

      g. Prior restraint, vagueness, and overbreadth

   3. Freedom of the press

   4. Freedom of association

Key Focus Areas for Constitutional Law

Judicial review, Separation of powers, Federal system, Individual rights

Introduction to Constitutional Law

Constitutional Law is the easiest area. However, on a multiple choice examination on Constitutional Law you can only test out well-settled principles of law and there are not that many well-settled principles, as you well know. If you get the basics down, it will be easy for you to score well on any constitutional law examination. You'll find several wrong answers to eliminate even if you don't know what the correct answer is.

One area that you want to pay particular attention to in your Constitutional Law review is the area of individual rights. The individual rights questions are some of the easiest. For instance, it will be perfectly obvious to you that somebody is suing because they claim that their individual rights have been violated. Your job is to say, "first of all, which individual right theory would they be suing under?"

In short, you must know the First Amendment and the individual rights rules to be successful on a constitutional law exam.

The areas under individual rights that are most heavily tested are:

1. Due process

2. Equal protection

3. The privileges and immunities clause of Article IV

4. The First Amendment. We can divide the First Amendment into two subcategories: (a) Free Speech and (b) Freedom of Religion.

Read the question below and use the IRAC method to answer it.

Approaching Constitutional Law Using IRAC

In an effort to protect the dwindling American bald eagle population, Congress has enacted the American Bald Eagle Preservation Act, which makes it illegal to take, possess, or sell any part of an

American bald eagle. The Act is challenged by Cliff, a seller of gifts that use American bald eagle feathers in them. Is the Act constitutional?

A. No, the statute violates due process because the absolute prohibition on scale is an effective taking under the Fifth Amendment Due Process Clause without just compensation.

B. No, because the statute is discriminatory as applied.

C. Yes, because the regulation is rationally related to interstate commerce.

D. Yes, because the statute is designed to protect a dwindling national resource.

IRAC Answer

Issue: We want to know whether the American Bald Eagle Preservation Act, which prohibits the possession or sale of any part of an American bald eagle, is constitutional or not.

Rule: It is evident that prohibiting the sale of anything using any part of an American bald eagle will affect commerce. Congress has enacted it under its broad commerce power.

Application: Here we must note that since the regulations do not compel surrender of the artifacts and there is no physical invasion, that there is no taking of a property right without just compensation.

Conclusion: Therefore, the correct answer is (C) since Congress' power to regulate is proper. Answer (A) is incorrect, (B) is not supported by the facts, and while (D) states the correct conclusion, it is for the wrong reasons.

∞ Constitutional Law Questions

Question 1

A state creates a policy prohibiting from voting any person who is a citizen of a country with which America is currently at war. Suriya is a dual citizen of America and Libya, and America is at war with Libya. Suriya is denied voting rights in the next state election. A federal law exists which denies states the right to deny citizens their rights based solely on issues of citizenship. Which of the following would be helpful in determining the constitutionality of the state policy?

A. The Privileges and Immunities Clause

B. The Equal Protection Clause

C. The Commerce Clause

D. The Supremacy Clause

Questions 2–5 Are Based on the Following

Kansas, a state in the heart of America's flatland, claims to be the motorcycle-riding capital of the country. To protect motorcyclists, Kansas passes a law requiring riders to wear helmets. Jim Small, a motorcycling enthusiast, doesn't like to wear the helmet because he can't feel the wind flowing in his long hair. However, Jim likes to ride in Kansas because the land is so flat. Jim sues the state of Kansas saying other motorists, such as car drivers or truckers, don't have wear helmets.

Question 2

What constitutional clause or amendment should Jim use to sue Kansas?

A. The Equal Protection Clause

B. The Due Process Clause

C. The Privacy Clause

D. The Taxing and Spending Powers

Question 3

Which scrutiny level of the Equal Protection clause would apply to the Kansas law?

A. Strict Scrutiny

B. Intermediate Scrutiny

C. Rational Basis

D. None of the above

Question 4

Based on your answer to Question 3, what is the test to be used to determine constitutionality in this case?

A. The law must be rationally related to a legitimate government activity.

B. The law must be substantially related to an important government objective.

C. The law must not conflict with a federal law.

D. The law must serve a compelling state interest.

Question 5

Applying the scrutiny test you chose in Question 4, is the Kansas law constitutional?

A. Yes, because motorist safety is a compelling state interest.

B. Yes, because motorist safety is a legitimate state interest.

C. No, because motorist safety is not an important government objective.

D. No, because Jim is not being discriminated against.

Question 6

Congress passes a law requiring that bicycle owners register them with a free federal bicycle registry. The purpose of the law is to provide reliable evidence of bicycle ownership to reduce bicycle theft, as more and more bicycles are being kept or resold in states *other* than the state where the bicycle was stolen. What part of the Constitution would help determine if this law is constitutional?

A. The Taxing and Spending Powers

B. The Commerce Clause

C. The First Amendment

D. State's Police Powers

Question 7

An ordinance by the city of Elba placed a $10 limit on individual contributions in support of or opposition to local political issues in the city. What constitutional provision helps determine the constitutionality of this ordinance?

A. The Privileges and Immunities Clause

B. The Due Process Clause

C. The Equal Protection Clause

D. First Amendment right to freedom of speech

Questions 8–9 Are Based on the Following

To encourage people to stop polluting the air, Congress passes a law taxing oxygen consumption and charges every adult person an amount based on the grams of oxygen they consume on a daily basis. This amount is calculated based on the adult person's height and weight. Tina Young, a 5 foot 1 inch, 250-pound woman, thinks this is unjust and sues the Federal government.

Question 8

What constitutional provision gives Congress the power to create such a law?

A. The separation of powers

B. The First Amendment

C. Judicial Review

D. The Commerce Clause

Question 9

What constitutional provision should Tina use to sue the Federal government?

    A. The Equal Protection Clause

    B. The Due Process Clause

    C. The Eleventh Amendment

    D. The Full Faith and Credit Clause

Question 10

Alabama passes a law preventing horse owners from "exercising, walking, or allowing the horse to use the bathroom" on any state owned land. Under the Judicial Review provisions of the Constitution, who would have proper standing to sue Alabama over the constitutionality of this law?

    A. A taxpaying citizen of Alabama.

    B. A federal judge.

    C. An Alabama horse owner.

    D. An Alabama horse owner who uses empty state owned land to walk his horse.

Contract Law Outline: Overview

Note: Examinees are to assume that Articles 1 of the Uniform Commercial Code as amended in 2001 and Article 2 as amended in 1999 are in effect. Applicants should assume that the 2003 proposed amendments to Article 2 have not been adopted. Approximately 60 percent of the Contracts questions for each MBE will be based on categories I, VII, and VIII, and approximately 40 percent will be based on the remaining categories, II, III, IV, V, VI, IX, and X. Approximately 25 percent of the Contracts questions for each MBE will be based on provisions of the Uniform Commercial Code, Articles 1 and 2.

I. FORMATION OF CONTRACTS

A. Mutual assent
  1. Offer and acceptance
  2. Mistake, misunderstanding, misrepresentation, nondisclosure, confidential relationship, fraud, undue influence, and duress
  3. Problems of communication and "battle of the forms"
  4. Indefiniteness or absence of terms
B. Capacity to contract
C. Illegality, unconscionability, and public policy
D. Implied-in-fact contract and quasi-contract
E. "Pre-contract" obligations based on detrimental reliance
F. Express and implied warranties in sale-of-goods contracts

II. CONSIDERATION

A. Bargain and exchange
B. "Adequacy" of consideration: mutuality of obligation, implied promises, and disproportionate exchanges
C. Modern substitutes for bargain: "moral obligation," detrimental reliance, and statutory substitutes
D. Modification of contracts: preexisting duties
E. Compromise and settlement of claims

III. THIRD-PARTY BENEFICIARY CONTRACTS

A. Intended beneficiaries
B. Incidental beneficiaries

    C. Impairment or extinguishment of third-party rights by contract modification or mutual rescission

    D. Enforcement by the promisee

IV. ASSIGNMENT OF RIGHTS AND DELEGATION OF DUTIES

V. STATUTES OF FRAUDS

VI. PAROL EVIDENCE AND INTERPRETATION

VII. CONDITIONS

    A. Express

    B. Constructive

        1. Conditions of exchange: excuse or suspension by material breach

        2. Immaterial breach and substantial performance

        3. Independent covenants

        4. Constructive conditions of non-prevention, non-hindrance, and affirmative cooperation

    C. Obligations of good faith and fair dealing in performance and enforcement of contracts

    D. Suspension or excuse of conditions by waiver, election, or estoppel

    E. Prospective inability to perform: effect on other party

VIII. REMEDIES

    A. Total and partial breach of contract

    B. Anticipatory repudiation

    C. Election of substantive rights and remedies

    D. Specific performance; injunction against breach; declaratory judgment

    E. Rescission and reformation

    F. Measure of damages in major types of contract and breach

    G. Consequential damages: causation, certainty, and foreseeability

    H. Liquidated damages and penalties

    I. Restitutionary and reliance recoveries

    J. Remedial rights of defaulting parties

    K. Avoidable consequences and mitigation of damages

IX. IMPOSSIBILITY OF PERFORMANCE AND FRUSTRATION OF PURPOSE

X. DISCHARGE OF CONTRACTUAL DUTIES

⚬ Key Focus Areas for Contract Law

Formation of Contracts, Conditions, Remedies, and Uniform Commercial Code Articles 1 and 2

∞ Introduction to Contract Law

In law, Contract is one of the most detailed areas. The one area in Contracts worth emphasizing is that of contract formation: offer, acceptance, and consideration. Direct most of your attention to understanding contract formation. It's not enough to know, for example, the general mailbox rule. You need to know the three or four variations on the general mailbox rule. In contract law, unless otherwise agreed or provided by law, acceptance of offer is effective when deposited in the mail if properly addressed. If you know the detailed rules, you will do well with this subject matter.

Following contract formation is third party beneficiaries; assignment of rights—delegation of duties; Article II, sales. Under sales, there are four key areas that you must fully understand:

1. Battle of the forms,
2. Contract modification without consideration,
3. Contract for the sale of goods—$5000 or more (which is both Common Law and part of Article II),
4. Sale of non-conforming goods.

Furthermore, Contract and Real Property fact patterns tend to be the longest and the most detailed. However, Real Property has fewer issues than Contracts.

The examiners will not include questions in which you can easily eliminate the wrong answers. They engage in word games, so you must read the four answer choices very carefully. Since the fact patterns are long and detailed, you must underline certain parts. You will be under pressure and will not have time to go back and re-read a long fact pattern.

You should always underline the following in Contracts:

1. The terms of the offer and the acceptance
2. Any dates
3. Any oral or telephonic communication
4. The subject matter and whether it's Article II. Always ask yourself "is this a contract for the sale of goods?" If it is, Article II applies. If it's a contract for anything else, common law applies. Normally, it will either be goods, which is Article II, or services.

∞ Approaching Contract Law Using IRAC

On Monday, Chad, a widget wholesaler, faxed Barney a letter promising to sell him 500 widgets for $2,000. On Tuesday, Barney telephoned Chad and said he was rejecting the offer because the price was too high. During the telephone conversation, Chad responded, "Why don't you wait and think it over until tomorrow?" The following day, Barney learned that there was a nationwide widget shortage. He immediately telephoned Chad and said, "I changed my mind and will accept your offer." Chad then told Barney, "Sorry, pal, you had your chance and blew it."

After Chad refused to sell the widgets to him, Barney sued for breach of contract. Is there an enforceable contract between the parties?

A. No, because Barney's telephone call on Tuesday constituted a rejection.

B. No, because there was no consideration to keep the offer open until Wednesday.

C. Yes, because Chad's statement "Why don't you think it over until tomorrow" revived the offer that Barney subsequently accepted in a timely fashion.

D. Yes, if and only if Chad and Barney are merchants.

IRAC Answer

Issue: Whether or not Chad's original offer to Barney is dead or was revived and open for Barney's acceptance.

Rule: According to Uniform Commercial Code 2-206 (UCC), "an offer to make a contract shall be construed as inviting acceptance in any manner and by any medium that is reasonable under the circumstances."

Application: Chad's statement "Why don't you think it over until tomorrow?" revived the original offer. It is also important to note that Barney's acceptance by telephone would be effective even though the offer was by a different medium.

Conclusion: "C" There are no magic words required to extend an offer, but all offers contain three elements: (1) An expression of intent to enter a present contract; (2) a sufficient articulation of the essential terms of the proposed bargain; and (3) communication of that intent and those terms to another person (the offeree) who has the capacity to form a contract by a timely and conforming acceptance. This contracts question deals with the revival of an offer. If, in the wake of a rejection/counter-offer, the offeror re-manifests an intention to trade on the terms of the original offer, that offer is once again open to an acceptance by the offeree.

Ref. PMBR Multistate Specialist "Early Bird" Workbook

Contract Law Questions

Questions 1–3 Are Based on the Following

Shane wanted to have a recording studio built in his house. He sent requests to local contractors, asking them to submit project bids. Roy submitted the lowest price bid, and Shane called him to find out what type of materials Roy's initial bid included. Shane asked Roy how much it would cost to substitute higher-quality materials and Roy agreed to check on the pricing for those superior materials. They also discussed a possible start date for the project. Immediately, Roy purchased the superior materials that Shane had asked about. Two weeks later, Shane changed his mind and decided not to build the studio. He called Roy to tell him the project was off. Roy filed a lawsuit against Shane for breach of contract.

Question 1

What are some of the key elements used to determine whether Roy's bid for the project was an offer?

A. Definiteness of terms and consideration

B. Serious intent, consideration, and definiteness of terms

C. Serious intent, definiteness of terms, and communication

D. Communication, adequacy of consideration, and fairness

Question 2

Was Shane's conduct and phone communication with Roy indicative of acceptance of Roy's bid?

A. No, the discussions between the two were preliminary negotiations. No final contract terms existed in the form of an offer for Shane to accept.

B. No, Shane rejected Roy's offer with his second phone call.

C. Yes, Shane's discussion of a starting date and inquiry into the materials he wanted showed his seriousness of intent to contract.

D. Yes, Shane should have never spoken to Roy, if he didn't want Roy to do the job.

Question 3

In the lawsuit, the court says there was not agreement between the two parties over this project, and therefore no contract. Roy, however, tries to recover for the cost of the superior materials that he purchased for Shane. What theory might help Roy recover those costs?

A. The Objective Theory of Contract

B. Promissory Estoppel

C. Charitable Subscriptions

D. The Mirror Image Rule

Questions 4–5 Are Based on the Following

John is a bicycle repairman who owns a small shop that he runs out of his garage. Driving by his neighbor's house, John sees a large metal shed for sale. John calls his neighbor and offers to buy it, which the neighbor accepts. John wants to dismantle the shed and move it to his own yard to use as a new bicycle shop. The neighbor offers to help John reassemble the shed in John's yard if John will help the neighbor dismantle the shed. John agrees and asks to make the move in 2 weeks. John helps the neighbor dismantle the shed, but the neighbor refuses to help John reassemble it. Once the shed is moved to John's yard, it takes John 4 weeks to reassemble it himself, and John loses several bicycle repair jobs.

Question 4

Is consideration present in the neighbor's promise to help John reassemble the shed?

A. No, because no additional money is exchanged.

B. No, because the economic value of the labor required to move the shed is not discussed.

C. Yes, because labor alone has legal value and was bargained for by John and the neighbor.

D. Yes, because the consideration given is fair.

Question 5

If John sues his neighbor to recover the profits he lost from the missed bicycle repair jobs, what contract theory might help him recover?

    A. Promissory Estoppel

    B. Accord and Satisfaction

    C. Covenant Not to Sue

    D. Preexisting Duty

Questions 6–8 Are Based on the Following

Val's Foods signs a contract to buy 1,000 pounds of tomatoes from Sun Farms, a small organic grower, as long as an independent organization inspects and certifies that the tomatoes have no pesticide residue. Val's has many contracts with local restaurants to supply them with tomatoes. Immediately before the tomato harvest at Sun Farms, an unexpected hailstorm destroys half of the tomato crop. Sun Farms tries to buy additional tomatoes from other farms, but it is too late in the season and the price of tomatoes is three times the normal market price. Sun Farms is too small to absorb the higher cost, so they cannot buy more tomatoes to fulfill their commitment to Val's. Sun Farms notifies Val's that it will not fulfill their performance duties.

Question 6

Suppose Sun Farms' tomatoes don't pass the pesticide residue inspection. What contract theory of conditions might allow Val's Foods to refuse contract performance?

    A. Rescission

    B. Material Alteration

    C. Discharge by Failure of Condition

    D. Accord and Satisfaction

Question 7

Under what contract theory of conditions might Sun Farms claim that its obligation under the contract has been discharged by operation of law?

    A. Frustration of Purpose

    B. Commercial Impracticability

    C. Temporary Impossibility

    D. Destruction of the Subject Matter

Question 8

Suppose Sun Farms contacts every organic tomato grower in the state and buys all of the last pesticide free tomatoes, but is only able to come up with 995 pounds in total. If Sun Farms gives the 995 pounds of tomatoes to Val's, under what contract theory would that satisfy Sun Farms' performance obligations?

A. Material Breach

B. Nonmaterial Breach

C. Novation

D. Substantial Performance

Questions 9–10 Are Based on the Following

Bruno contracted with Xtreme Productions to be a stuntman in Xtreme's movies. Bruno is known in the acting industry as the best stuntman, and Xtreme produces only intense action movies with a lot of high speed chases and stunts. Filming on a new movie is set to begin on August 1 and end on December 1 so that the film will be ready for release the following summer, when it can make the most profits. Bruno's contract stipulates that filming must follow this time schedule. The contract also says that Bruno will be paid 10 % net profit from the summer movie release in addition to his salary. The contract has a liquidated damages clause saying if Bruno breaks the contract, he will owe Xtreme $1 million. The contract has a limited liability clause saying if Bruno is injured during his stunts, Xtreme will only be liable for nominal damages.

Question 9

What factors would a court consider to determine whether the $1 million liquidated damages clause is enforceable?

A. At the time of contracting, was it apparent that damages would be hard to establish if a breach occurred?

B. Was the amount set as damages a reasonable estimate of potential damages?

C. A and B

D. Neither A nor B

Question 10

Suppose Bruno's contract had no liquidated damages clause and Xtreme breached the contract, causing the film release to be delayed until the fall of the next year. What type of remedy could Bruno seek for lost profits from the movie not being released during the summer?

A. Consequential Damages

B. Punitive Damages

C. Specific Performance

D. Unjust Enrichment

Criminal Law Outline: Overview

Approximately 40% of the Criminal Law questions for each MBE will be based on category V, and approximately 60% will be based on the remaining categories, I through IV.

I. HOMICIDE

A. Intended killings

    1. Premeditation-deliberation

    2. Provocation

B. Unintended killings

    1. Intent to injure

    2. Reckless and negligent killings

    3. Felony-murder

    4. Misdemeanor-manslaughter

II. OTHER CRIMES

A. Theft

    1. Larceny

    2. Embezzlement

    3. False pretenses

B. Receiving stolen goods

C. Robbery

D. Burglary

E. Assault and battery

F. Rape; statutory rape

G. Kidnapping

H. Arson

I. Possession offenses

III. INCHOATE CRIMES; PARTIES

A. Inchoate offenses

    1. Attempts

    2. Conspiracy

    3. Solicitation

B. Parties to crime

IV. General principles
A. Acts and omissions
B. State of mind
   1. Required mental state
   2. Strict liability
   3. Mistake of fact or law
C. Responsibility
   1. Mental disorder
   2. Intoxication
D. Causation
E. Justification and excuse
F. Jurisdiction

V. Constitutional protection of accused persons
A. Arrest, search and seizure
B. Confessions and privilege against self-incrimination
C. Lineups and other forms of identification
D. Right to counsel
E. Fair trial and guilty pleas
F. Double jeopardy
G. Cruel and unusual punishment
H. Burdens of proof and persuasion

Key Focus Areas for Criminal Law

Crimes, Homicides, Criminal Procedure, Inchoate Crimes and Parties, General principles, Constitutional Protection of the Accused Person

Introduction to Criminal Law

Criminal Law requires the memorization of offenses and their elements. Criminal procedure can be fairly easy. Testing in this area will generally focus on warning-type issues, search and seizure, and right to counsel. In the case of burglary, for example, memorize its elements always focusing on intent since that is the main one students miss. Intent is very important in criminal law.

The following is a short outline to use as a mental checklist on the examination. There are three possibilities for intent in Criminal Law cases:

1. **Specific Intent:** requires proof that a person had the specific intent to commit that crime. The four categories of specific intent crimes are
   a. All fact offenses
   b. Solicitation, conspiracy, attempt. Underline attempt because it is the most important, the one that is often missed, and the one always tested on.
   c. First-degree murder
   d. Assault with intent to commit a battery

The last two are the least emphasized. You should know what the four categories of specific intent are and be able to identify them on an exam. When you come to a Criminal Law question, determine the intent for the crime and then write it in the margin. This applies to all the offenses, not just burglary or larceny, but also to crimes such as false pretenses.

In addition, there are two initial defenses that apply only to specific intent crimes. They are

    a. Voluntary intoxication
    b. Any mistake of fact, even an unreasonable one

2. **Malice Crimes:** arson and murder. The test for malice is recklessness or extreme indifference to human life. Unlike the category of specific intent, in the case of a malice crime there is no need to prove intent—only extreme recklessness.
3. **General Intent Crimes:** all other crimes. Any crime that is neither specific intent nor malice is a general intent crime.

Note: The following was transcribed from Clarkson, Miller, Jentz, and Cross West's Business Law. Ohio: Thomson, 2006

When we think about Criminal Law, we probably think about ways in which people can be punished for committing crimes against society. American values make us understand that our system is based on laws that have been created by our legislatures that shape the rules for society and are supposed to apply to everyone. These laws set the standards for our behavior and we know that when these laws are broken, there are consequences.

Since the state has extensive resources at its disposal when prosecuting criminal cases, there are numerous procedural safeguards to protect the rights of defendants. We look here at one of these safeguards—the higher burden of proof that applies in a criminal case—as well as the harsher sanctions for criminal acts compared with civil wrongs.

Burden of Proof—In a civil case, the plaintiff usually must prove his or her case by a preponderance of the evidence (slightly more than 50%). Under this standard, the plaintiff must convince the court that based on the evidence presented by both parties; it is more likely than not that the plaintiff's allegations are true. In a criminal case, in contrast, the state must prove its case beyond a reasonable doubt. If the jury views the evidence in the case as reasonably permitting a guilty or a not guilty verdict, then the jury's verdict must be not guilty. The higher burden of proof in criminal cases reflects a fundamental social value—the belief that it is worse to convict an innocent individual than to let a guilty person go free. The table below better summarizes the key differences between civil law and criminal law.

Key Differences between Civil and Criminal Law		
ISSUE	**CIVIL LAW**	**CRIMINAL LAW**
Party who brings suit	Person who suffered harm	The State
Wrongful Act	Causing harm to a person or to a person's property	Violating a statute that prohibits some type of activity
Burden of proof	Preponderance of the evidence	Beyond a reasonable doubt
Verdict	Three-fourths majority (typically)	Unanimous
Remedy	Damages to compensate for the harm or a decree to achieve an equitable result	Punishment (fine, imprisonment, or death)

Two elements must exist for a person to be convicted of a crime: (1) the performance of a prohibited act and (2) a specified state of mind, or intent, on the part of the actor. Additionally, to establish criminal liability, there must be a *concurrence* (agreement) between the act and the intent.

The Criminal Act—In criminal law, a prohibited act is referred to as the **actus reus**, or guilty act. In some cases an act of omission can be a crime, but only when a person has legal duty to perform the omitted act, such as filing a tax return.

State of Mind—A wrongful mental state, **mens rea** is also typically required to establish criminal liability. The mental state, or intent, is indicated in the applicable statute or law. Murder, for example, involves the guilty act of killing another human being, and the mental state is the desire, or intent, to take another's life. When analyzing criminal law problems, students must always look for these two major elements: Guilty Mind and Guilty Act (*mens rea*) and (*actus rea*).

Criminal Law is guided by laws (Substantive Law) and legal procedures (Procedural Law) that are the major elements that shape the criminal justice system.

Substantive Criminal Law

These are the laws that define acts subject to punishment and make specific the punishment for such offenses. It is often called the penal code and it answers the question of "What is illegal?"

Procedural Criminal Law

These are the laws that define the procedures criminal justice officials must follow in enforcement, determining if defendant is guilty or not guilty, and corrections. It answers the question of "How the law shall be enforced."

∞ Approaching Criminal Law Using IRAC

Anglo-American criminal law is founded upon certain basic premises that courts and legislatures have more or less strictly observed when formulating the substantive law of crimes. These basic premises concern the requirements of (1) act, (2) mental state, (3) concurrence, (4) harm, (5) causation, (6) punishment and 7) legality. The first of these basic premises concerns the requirement of an act. As a general rule, it is commonly held that conduct, to be criminal, must consist of something more than a mere "bad state of mind."

With regard to the requirement of an act, in which of the following cases would the defendant, if charged with criminal homicide, most likely be acquitted because there was no act?

A. Aaron was a chronic sleepwalker. On Monday, Aaron got into a violent argument with his next-door neighbor, Sidney. The next night, while he was asleep, Aaron left his home and walked to Sidney's house. He entered the front door, which was unlocked, and ascended the stairs to Sidney's bedroom. While still sleepwalking, Aaron went inside and strangled Sidney to death.

B. Bernie suffered from an incurable malignant brain tumor. One night he stabbed his roommate, Reggie, to death. Bernie later stated that he could remember the occurrence clearly. A physician testified that Bernie's brain tumor could at times deprive him of his ability to control his movements.

C. Cassandra was an epileptic who had experienced seizures in the past. As she was driving to work one morning, she had an epileptic seizure. As a result, she lost control of her vehicle, which went through a red light and struck a group of school children crossing the street. The accident killed two young girls.

D. Dozer, a drug addict, injected himself with a speedball, containing a mixture of heroin and cocaine. A few seconds later, Dozer began to hallucinate. Believing that he was a rabid dog, Dozer attacked his girlfriend, Giselle, and bit off her nose and ears. Giselle died from her wounds.

IRAC Answer

Issue: Whether or not the defendant's state of mind precluded his behavior from being classified as an intentional act.

Rule: Bad thought alone cannot constitute a crime; there must be an act, or an omission to act, where there is a legal duty to act. Thus, common law crimes are defined in terms of an act or an omission to act, and statutory crimes are unconstitutional unless so defined.

Application: Here the accused was sleepwalking. According to criminal law expert LaFave, "one is not guilty of murder if he killed the victim while asleep or in the clouded state between sleeping and walking."

Conclusion: "A" Even assuming that "the conduct of a sleepwalker may be purposive (though not recollected on waking), and may be regarded as expressing unconscious desire," it is nonetheless undoubtedly sound not to impose liability for an unconscious desire that manifests in this way.

Criminal Law Questions

Questions 1–2 Are Based on the Following

Ed Hand worked for a railroad company as a roadmaster responsible for every detail of the safe and efficient maintenance and construction of the track, structures, projects, and marine facilities of the entire railroad line. The railroad had a special rock-quarry project that ran above an oil pipeline along the track. One day, the quarry's backhoe operator punctured the pipeline, which he was unaware of, spilling 5,000 gallons of oil into a nearby river. Hand was charged with the crime of negligent discharge of harmful substances under the Clean Water Act.

Question 1

Did Hand have the required mental state for conviction of the accused crime?

   A. No, because he didn't puncture the pipeline.

   B. No, because he didn't mean to pollute the river.

   C. Yes, because he meant to pollute the river.

   D. Yes, because he was in charge of the project and had the power to prevent the act.

Question 2

Could the backhoe operator also be charged with the same crime as Hand?

 A. No, because he is missing the mens rea element of the crime.

 B. No, because he is missing the actus reus element of the crime.

 C. Yes, because he is the actual person who caused the oil spill.

 D. Yes, because he knew the oil pipeline was there and was reckless.

Question 3

As Maria is walking home from work, a man in a face mask points a gun to her head and demands that Maria give him her purse and jewelry. She is unharmed and immediately calls the police, who catch the man on the next block. The man should be charged with the crime of:

 A. Theft

 B. Burglary

 C. Robbery

 D. Receiving stolen goods

Question 4

Eric is a certified scuba diver and diving hobbyist. His best friend Jamon, who recently started dating Eric's ex-girlfriend, wants to go diving with Eric. Eric agrees and sees the dive as an opportunity to get back at Jamon. Eric knows that it is impossible for a human to dive without oxygen for more than 12 minutes at a time, but he turns off Jamon's oxygen while he is under water for 11½? minutes. Jamon does not survive the dive. Eric claims he never meant to kill Jamon. What crime is Eric guilty of?

 A. Murder

 B. Attempted Murder

 C. Assault

 D. Battery

Question 5

Terry has lived with his partner, Gene, for 30 years. Gene has stage four pancreatic cancer that has spread to his liver, lungs, and brain. Doctors have given Gene 2 months to live, but Gene is in terrible pain and begs Terry to end his life for him. Terry attempts to poison Gene with overdoses of prescription painkillers and Gene dies within 3 days. However, an autopsy shows that Gene died of cancer, not of poisoning. Why might Terry be acquitted of the crime of murder?

 A. There is no actus reus of murder in Terry's actions.

 B. There is no mens rea of murder in Terry's actions.

C. Gene had consented to Terry's actions.

D. Terry was insane.

Question 6

Aimee is arrested and tried in her home state for grand theft auto. The trial jury cannot come to a majority consensus of her guilt or non-guilt, so they are a hung jury. The state dismisses the jury and schedules a retrial of Aimee for the same crime 2 weeks later. Has the state used double jeopardy against Aimee?

A. Yes, the Constitution says the government can't try the same person more than once.

B. Yes, a hung jury is the same result as a not guilty verdict.

C. No, double jeopardy only attaches after a non-guilty verdict is given.

D. No, double jeopardy only applies to aggravated crimes, which Aimee's crime was not.

Question 7

Dylan is arrested at his home and read his Miranda Rights properly under the law. After his Rights are read to him, Dylan states that he wants to waive his Rights. What state of mind does Dylan have to be in to make a waiver of Miranda Rights effective?

A. Sober

B. Knowing and Loud

C. Knowing and Persuasive

D. Knowing and Intelligent

Questions 8–9 Are Based on the Following

Jamie has a key to his father's electronics store warehouse, because he is an assistant manager at the store. One night, Jamie uses the key to open the warehouse and steals a laptop computer. Jamie sells stolen laptop to Phyllis, who buys it cheap because she knows it is stolen. Phyllis then gives the laptop to her niece, Samantha as an 18th birthday present.

Question 8

Which of these people is guilty of a crime?

A. Jamie

B. Jamie and Phyllis

C. Jamie, Phyllis, and Samantha

D. Phyllis

Question 9

Jamie is guilty of stealing the laptop, but is he guilty of burglary?

- **A.** No, because his entry into the warehouse was lawful.

- **B.** No, because his father gave him a key.

- **C.** Yes, because he had an intent to steal something in the warehouse.

- **D.** Yes, because he actually committed a felony in the warehouse.

Question 10

Lee and Smith conspire to set up a fake charity to solicit donations for children in need. Instead of giving money to the children, they would keep the donations for themselves. They make brochures about the charity and mail them to prospective donors. They also spend many hours calling prospective donors to request charitable contributions. Lee's wife finds out about their scheme and threatens to tell the police unless they immediately close it down. Lee offers to give his wife 30% of the donations if she doesn't tell anyone about the scheme, but before he can give her the money, one of the donors becomes suspicious and reports them to the government. What group of crimes is Lee guilty of?

- **A.** Mail fraud, wire fraud, and theft.

- **B.** Mail fraud, wire fraud, and bribery.

- **C.** Mail fraud, bribery, and theft.

- **D.** Mail fraud, wire fraud, theft, and bribery.

Evidence Law Outline: Overview

Approximately one-third of the Evidence questions for each MBE will be based on category I, one-third on category V, and one-third on the remaining categories, II, III, and IV.

I. PRESENTATION OF EVIDENCE

A. Introduction of evidence
1. Requirement of personal knowledge
2. Refreshing recollection
3. Objections and offers of proof
4. Lay opinions
5. Competency of witnesses
6. Judicial notice
7. Roles of judge and jury
8. Limited admissibility
9. Contradiction

B. Presumptions

C. Mode and order
1. Control by court
2. Scope of examination
3. Form of questions
4. Exclusion of witnesses

D. Impeachment, contradiction, and rehabilitation
1. Inconsistent statements and conduct
2. Bias and interest
3. Conviction of crime
4. Specific instances of conduct
5. Character for truthfulness
6. Ability to observe, remember, or relate accurately
7. Impeachment of hearsay declarants
8. Rehabilitation of impeached witnesses

E. Proceedings to which evidence rules apply

II. RELEVANCY AND REASONS FOR EXCLUDING RELEVANT EVIDENCE

    A. Probative value
        1. Relevancy
        2. Exclusion for unfair prejudice, confusion, or waste of time
    B. Authentication and identification
    C. Character and related concepts
        1. Admissibility of character
        2. Methods of proving character
        3. Habit and routine practice
        4. Other crimes, acts, transactions, and events
        5. Prior sexual misconduct of a defendant
    D. Expert testimony
        1. Qualifications of witnesses
        2. Bases of testimony
        3. Ultimate issue rule
        4. Reliability and relevancy
        5. Proper subject matter
    E. Real, demonstrative, and experimental evidence

III. PRIVILEGES AND OTHER POLICY EXCLUSIONS

    A. Spousal immunity and marital communications
    B. Attorney-client and work product
    C. Physician/psychotherapist-patient
    D. Self-incrimination
    E. Other privileges
    F. Insurance coverage
    G. Remedial measures
    H. Compromise, payment of medical expenses, and plea negotiations
    I. Past sexual conduct of a victim

IV. WRITINGS, RECORDINGS, AND PHOTOGRAPHS

    A. Requirement of original
    B. Summaries
    C. Completeness rule

V. HEARSAY AND CIRCUMSTANCES OF ITS ADMISSIBILITY

    A. Definition of hearsay
        1. What is hearsay
        2. Prior statements by witness
        3. Statements attributable to party-opponent
        4. Multiple hearsay

B. Present sense impressions and excited utterances

C. Statements of mental, emotional, or physical condition

D. Statements for purposes of medical diagnosis and treatment

E. Past recollection recorded

F. Business records

G. Public records and reports

H. Learned treatises

I. Former testimony; depositions

J. Statements against interest

K. Other exceptions to the hearsay rule

L. Right to confront witnesses

Key Focus Areas for Evidence Law

Presentation of Evidence, Relevancy, Privileges, and writings and hearsay

Introduction to Evidence Law

The law of evidence is a system of rules and standards by which the admission of proof at the trial of a lawsuit is regulated. The material facts in the controversy are determined by proof that is filtered through the applicable rules of evidence. This proof includes testimony, writings, physical objects, and anything else presented to the senses of the jury.

The following areas must be given special attention and must be fully understood:

- Privileges: attorney-client privileges, physician-patient privileges, and spousal privileges
- Hearsay, non-hearsay, and hearsay exceptions are very important
- Impeachment
- Character evidence in both civil and criminal cases

The most important and most difficult area in Evidence Law is Character Evidence. The following is a summary of some heavily tested Character Evidence rules that will help you remember the rules. Using this framework will also help you answer the first questions here on Evidence. The rules for Evidence depend on whether they are applied to criminal case or civil case.

Character Evidence in Criminal Cases

1. Character Evidence is inadmissible[3] if offered by P (Prosecutor) to show that D (Defendant) has a propensity[4] to commit crimes.

2. Character Evidence is admissible[5] if offered by the D to show character not in keeping with the offense charged.

[3] Inadmissible—not allowed

[4] Propensity—tendency

[5] Admissible—allowed

a. The evidence that is admitted by calling another witness to testify is limited to opinion or reputation.

b. The evidence that is rebutted by calling a rebuttal witness to testify is limited to opinion or reputation as well.

Character Evidence in Civil Cases

1. It is inadmissible if offered by either party to show that either party acted in conformity with that character trait.
2. It is admissible if character itself is at issue:
   a. Defamation, which you see 98% of the time in the testing of this doctrine
   b. Negligent Hiring
   c. Negligent Entrustment

Character Evidence in Both Criminal and Civil Cases

One problem students have in determining which rule to apply on exams is knowing whether hearsay is involved. When a question asks, "Is this statement admissible?" the correct response is that there are three possible theories. Is the issue impeachment; relevancy, which is usually character evidence; or hearsay? In this case, use the process of elimination; if it's not character evidence and not impeachment evidence, then it must be hearsay.

However, examiners sometimes include confusing information. For example, the issue may be a hearsay exception dying declaration, but none of the answer choices deal with dying declaration. Instead, three choices include rules that sound familiar, but deal with impeachment rather than hearsay. The fourth answer simply says, "The testimony is admissible assuming this is a credible witness." Eliminating the three answers with tangible rules, you are left with the only possible correct answer, which really says nothing at all: evidence is admissible if the witness is credible. Circle the answer and move on.

Be aware, too, that examiners sometimes change one or two words in a rule, so that it sounds right but is actually incorrect.

∞ Approaching Evidence Law Using IRAC

Dryden is tried on a charge of driving while intoxicated. When Dryden was booked at the police station, the police made a videotape that showed him unsteady, abusive and speaking in a slurred manner. If the prosecutor lays a foundation properly indentifying the tape, should the court admit it in evidence and permit it to be shown to the jury?

A. Yes, because it is an admission.

B. Yes, because unfair prejudice does not substantially outweigh its probative value.

C. No, because the privilege against self-incrimination is applicable.

D. No, because extrinsic evidence cannot prove specific instances of conduct.

IRAC Answer

Issue: Whether or not the video tape of Dryden the Defendant is relevant admissible evidence.

Rule: Under Federal Rules of Evidence (F.R.E.) 401, relevant evidence is that which tends to make the existence of a fact of consequence more (or less) probable than it would otherwise be. Relevant evidence is generally admissible (F.R.E. 402), but it is inadmissible where its probative value is outweighed by the danger of unfair prejudice, confusion of the issues, misleading the jury or by considerations of undue delay, waste of time or needless presentation of cumulative evidence (F.R.E. 403).

Application: The videotape of Dryden showing him unsteady, abusive and speaking in a slurred manner is relevant on a charge of driving while intoxicated and should be admitted. It is neither prejudicial nor unfair to Dryden.

Conclusion: "B"

Evidence Law Questions

Question 1

Lydia and her brother, Sam, are in business together selling imported goods. Lydia tries to get her contact in Indonesia to steal goods instead of paying for them. Sam overhears this conversation and refuses to do business with her anymore. Sam also tells all their family about Lydia's phone call and that she was sleeping with her Indonesian contact, too. Lydia was not sleeping with her Indonesian contact. When Lydia sues Sam for slander in defamation, what evidence will be allowed?

A. The conversation overhead by the business's secretary.

B. Lydia's worldwide travel record.

C. Proof of Lydia's good or bad character.

D. A conversation about the case between Lydia and her attorney.

Question 2

Devin is charged with child molestation. At Devin's trial, what type of character evidence will be admissible?

A. Evidence of Devin's good behavior with children, including his past experience as a day care worker and babysitter, with testimony from the day care owner and his babysitting clients about how he is a great caregiver of children.

B. Evidence from Devin's neighbor, who will testify that she overhead Devin telling his friend how he "loves little girls."

C. Evidence from the prosecution showing that Devin has been charged with other non-child-related crimes in the past, even though he was never convicted of those crimes.

D. Evidence of Devin's physical health records.

Question 3

Emma and Richard are husband and wife. Richard has been charged with tax evasion, and in seeking out evidence of this crime, the state prosecution finds evidence of Richard fraudulently transferring $100,000 of his employer's money to his wife. The state wants Emma and Richard to submit to depositions to question them about this transfer. Emma refuses, invoking the spousal privilege, which allows conversations between spouses not to be admitted as evidence. Will the court allow Emma's privilege to stand?

- **A.** No, because she waived the right to the privilege when her husband committed a crime.
- **B.** No, because the spousal privilege cannot be used when a third party is defrauded.
- **C.** Yes, because she is the not accused person, her husband is the accused person.
- **D.** Yes, because the spousal privilege always stands.

Question 4

Sylvano files a negligence lawsuit against Ryah for injuries he sustained while Ryah was speeding down the street in her car and ran over Sylvano's toe. Ryah denies that she was driving on the street at the time Sylvano claims he was injured. George was walking down the street at the time and saw the event take place as Sylvano described it, which he testified to in a deposition right after the accident. Six months later, at trial, Sylvano calls George to the stand to testify that he saw Ryah on the street the day of his accident. George, however, states that he had never seen Ryah before. Sylvano's attorney wants to show George's deposition statements to impeach George's trial testimony. Will evidence of George's deposition be admissible?

- **A.** No, because a party cannot impeach his own witness.
- **B.** No, because the deposition is hearsay.
- **C.** Yes, because a party can impeach his own witness.
- **D.** Yes, because the deposition is material to the case.

Question 5

Kenya and Chloe are talking about a criminal scam arrangement. Margot overhears their conversation as she passes by them on the sidewalk. When Kenya and Chloe are brought to trial for the crime, the prosecutor finds out about Margot and wants her to testify in court. Would her testimony be allowed?

- **A.** Yes, because she was an "eyewitness" to the crime.
- **B.** Yes, because her testimony would confirm the crime.
- **C.** No, because her testimony is irrelevant.
- **D.** No, because her testimony is hearsay.

Property Law Outline: Overview

Approximately 75% of the Real Property questions for each MBE will be based on categories I, II, and V, and approximately 25% will be based on the remaining categories, III and IV. All of the major topics (designated by Roman numerals) will be represented in each examination, but not necessarily all of the subtopics.

Note: For all the topics listed in the outline below, the following matters are included, to the extent relevant:

- Nature and characteristics
- Creation
- Classification of interests
- Rights of possession and use
- Legal and equitable remedies

I. OWNERSHIP
- **A.** Present estates
   1. Fees simple
   2. Defeasible fees simple
   3. Life estates
- **B.** Cotenancy
   1. Tenancy in common
   2. Joint tenancy
- **C.** Future interests
   1. Reversions
   2. Remainders, vested and contingent
   3. Executory interests
   4. Possibilities of reverter, powers of termination
- **D.** The law of landlord and tenant
   1. Fitness and suitability of premises
   2. Types of holdings: creation and termination
      a. Terms for years
      b. Tenancies at will

      c. Holdovers and other tenancies at sufferance

      d. Periodic tenancies

    3. Assignment and subletting

    4. Rent

    5. Surrender, mitigation of damages, and anticipatory breach

  E. Special problems

    1. Rule Against Perpetuities

    2. Alienability, descendability, and devisability

II. RIGHTS IN LAND

  A. Covenants at law and in equity

  B. Easements, profits, and licenses

  C. Other interests in land

    1. Fixtures (including relevant application of Article 9, UCC)

    2. Scope and extent of real property

      a. Superjacent, adjacent, and subjacent space

      b. Rights in the common resources of light, air, streams, and bodies of water

      c. Nuisance

  D. Taking and aspects of zoning

III. REAL PROPERTY CONTRACT

  A. Relationships included

    1. Contracts to buy and sell by conveyance of realty

    2. Installment contract

  B. Creation and construction

    1. Statute of Frauds

    2. Essential terms

    3. Implied conditions or terms

      a. Time for performance

      b. Title required

      c. Burdens related to title defects

  C. Performance

    1. Fitness and suitability of premises

    2. Marketable title

    3. Risk of loss

  D. Interests before conveyance

    1. Equitable conversion

    2. Earnest-money deposits

  E. Relationships after conveyance

    1. Condition of premises

    2. Title problems

IV. **REAL PROPERTY MORTGAGES**
   A. Types of security devices
      1. Mortgages (including deeds of trust)
      2. Land contracts as security device
      3. Absolute deeds as security
   B. Some security relationships
      1. Necessity and nature of obligation
      2. Theories: title, lien, and intermediate
      3. Rights and duties prior to foreclosure
      4. Right to redeem and clogging equity of redemption
   C. Transfers by mortgagor
      1. Distinguishing "subject to" and "assuming"
      2. Rights and obligations of transferror
      3. Application of subrogation and suretyship principles
      4. Due-on-sale clauses
   D. Transfers by mortgagee (including effect of Article 3 of UCC)
   E. Discharge and defenses
   F. Foreclosure
      1. Types
      2. Rights of omitted parties
      3. Deficiency and surplus
      4. Redemption after foreclosure
      5. Deed in lieu of foreclosure

V. **TITLES**
   A. Adverse possession
   B. Conveyancing by deed
      1. Types
      2. Necessity for a grantee
      3. Delivery (including escrows)
      4. Land description and boundaries
      5. Covenants for title
   C. Conveyancing by will
      1. Ademption
      2. Exoneration
      3. Lapse
   D. Priorities and recording
      1. Types of priority
         a. Recording acts
         b. Judgment liens
         c. Fraudulent conveyances
         d. Protection of bona fide purchasers other than under statutes

2. Scope of coverage
    a. Recorded documents
    b. Elements required
    c. Parties protected
    d. Interests affected
3. Special problems
    a. After acquired title (including estoppel by deed)
    b. Constructive notice
    c. Forged instruments
    d. Transfers by corporations and by agents
    e. Purchase money mortgages

Introduction to Property Law

The Real Property questions are long and tedious. They are not as difficult as the Contract questions because Real Property questions deal normally with one single issue. There will be several facts in the question. By identifying what the issue is and applying the rules of law to that particular issue, it becomes relatively easy.

Begin by reading over the fact pattern, which normally identifies the issue at hand. Knowing what the issue is, it is usually simple to figure out who the winning party is and what they will be awarded from the court. The answer should then be easily found within the given choices.

You will not have time to go back and re-read entire Real Property fact patterns. Instead, underline the following key issues and facts as well as other facts you consider important.

- The language from the conveyance, or what we transfer the property with: the deed or the will. If this information is included, it will be important.
- Any dates, as they will usually be significant.
- A reference to the rule against perpetuities *might* be a factor in the problem.

Real Property is straightforward; it is simply a test of your memorization of the black letter law. Pay close attention to the recording statutes and mortgages.

Property Law is defined as the area of law that concentrates on the possession of real property (immovable property) and personal property (movable property). Property law also protects the rights of possession, enjoyment, and disposal within the bounds of real and personal property. It is important to understand the differences between real property and personal property when applying the rights and obligations of law.

Five Key Areas That Help Define Type of Property Law

1. *Acquisition of property* involves giving land as a gift; adverse possession; deeds; lost, mislaid, and abandoned property; bailment and license.

    Gift: In order for a gift to be legally effective, the grantor must have intended to give the gift to the grantee. Furthermore, the gift must be received and accepted by the grantee.

Property can be gifted *inter vivos* (during life), *mortis* (after death), or *causa mortis* (gift not effective until death).

Adverse Possession: Title of another's property by the continued use of the property that conflicts with the true owner's rights for a specified period of time.

Deeds: Legal way to grant rights to property.

Lost, mislaid, or abandoned property: personal property that has left the possession of the rightful owner without having directly entered the possession of another.

Bailment: The transfer of possession from bailor to bailee; however, it is not the transfer of ownership.

License: Permission given to another to enter or use property.

2. *Estates in land* involve fee simple, life estate, future interest, concurrent interest, and leasehold estates.

Fee simple: The absolute ownership of real property limited by the government powers of taxation, eminent domain, police power and escheat; may also be subject to conditions in the deed.

Life estate: Ownership of land for the duration of a person's life.

Future Interest: Legal right of property that does not include the present possession or enjoyment of the property.

Concurrent interest: Property owned by more than one person at a given time. Also known as co-tenancy.

Leasehold estate: Ownership or interest in land held by a tenant or lessee by some form of title issued by the lessor or landlord.

3. *Conveyance of interest* in land involves estoppel by deed, quitclaim deed, and mortgage.

Estoppel by deed: The grantor gives an implied covenant that title will be conveyed to the grantee; therefore, the grantee can sue to compel the transfer of title from the grantor.

Quitclaim deed: Document by which a person disclaims any interest the grantor has in the property, and passes claim to another person. This type of deed does not certify that the claim in the land in actually valid.

Mortgage: Using real or personal property as security for the payment of debt.

4. *Limiting control over future use* of land involves many different areas. The one on which to concentrate is the rule of perpetuities.

Rule of perpetuities: Prevents a property from being controlled mortmain or by "dead hand."

5. *Non-possessory interest* in land involves easements, profit, and covenants.

Easements: The right to do or prevent something over the real property of another.

Types of easements: easement in gross, easement appurtenant, prescriptive easement

Extinguish easements: An easement can either be terminated through the expiration of its term as determined upon its creation or by one of several events occurring subsequent to creation. Events that can extinguish an easement include these: (1) the same individual becoming the owner of the dominant as well as the servient estate when an appurtenant easement existed; (2) the owner of an easement in gross obtaining ownership of the servient estate; (3) the owner of the dominant tenement executing a deed or will releasing the easement in favor of the owner of the servient tenement; and (4) the abandonment of an easement.[6]

Profit: The right to take natural resources (minerals, timber, game, etc.) from the land of another. Non-possessory interest contains an implied easement.

Covenant: An agreement of adjoining landowners to do or refrain from doing something with relation to the land.

∞ Approaching Property Law Using IRAC

As you read earlier, IRAC is a method used to approach a legal issue that breaks down the facts and case and allows for critical examination. Using this method can help you answer any question dealing with property law.

1. **Issue.** Spot the issue at hand. Read the facts and the question—several times if needed. Make sure to spot both the facts laid out as well as the question that is being asked. If there is more than one issue laid out, order them in the most logical way possible.

2. **Rule.** Identify the rule to be used in answering the issue at hand. Make sure that you know the rule, as well as how it is used and the limitations. Often, a particular rule will seem to fit, but the scope of the issue will lie outside the scope of the rule, so know the rule's limitations. Try to be as specific as possible with the rule. Think about the exceptions to the rule. The question may contain the rule, but the rule may only be applied through the exceptions to the specific rule. For example, if the question asks about the fee simple, do not write everything you know about the possession of real property. Keep it relevant to the issue.

3. **Application.** After you decide on the rule to be used, you must apply it to the issue. Try to think and reason in the most logical order possible. How should the rule be applied to this situation? Try to understand the reasoning behind the rule and how it is applied.

4. **Conclusion.** Summarize your findings and a possible explanation to the application of the rule. Consider remedies and the positions of other parties.

Read the question below and apply the IRAC method:

Franklin owned 600 acres of land he inherited from his late uncle. One half of the property was densely wooded, and the other half was occupied by a large gravel pit. Until his death, Franklin's Uncle Thomas owned and operated Tom's Sand and Gravel. Thomas had thought about cutting and selling the timber on the land but had not done so by the time of his death.

Two years after Thomas' death, Franklin transferred title to his daughter Mary for life, with the remainder going to the State Tree Trust for Historic Preservation.

Mary wants to continue to run the sand and gravel business and to cut and sell the trees. Tree Trust, the holder of the remainder, sues to block Mary on the theory of waste.

How will the court most likely rule?

A. Tree Trust can stop both the gravel mining and the tree cutting.

B. Tree Trust can stop neither the gravel mining nor the tree cutting.

C. Tree Trust can stop the tree cutting but not the gravel mining.

D. Tree Trust can stop the gravel mining but not the tree cutting.

IRAC Answer

Issue: Is the exploitation of natural resources permitted if the land is designated as a life estate?

Rule: Life Estate ownership rights (ownership of land for the duration of one's life subject to limitations) with the limitation of waste (devaluing the land or damaging the land).

Application: In this case, Mary has been issued the land via life estate, which allows her the rights to the enjoyment of the land for as long as her life. However, the life estate is restricted by the creation of waste. There exists an understood use of the gravel mining pit, which was associated with a mining business and that could continue to be used; however, the trees were not a part of the business and the grantor had no intent to permit the cutting of timber.

Conclusion: The application of the rule prohibits answer choices A, B, and D from being correct, leaving C to be the only probable solution to the problem.

∞ Real Property Questions

Question 1

Frank and Fiona are husband and wife looking for a home. They fall in love with an empty home owned by Gustav and offer him $200,000 cash for it. Gustav agrees with a handshake and asks Frank to deliver a cashier's check in that amount the following week. Fiona immediately starts moving into the home, and tears out old floorboards and wall fixtures to make room for new ones. When Frank tries to deliver the cashier's check to Gustav, Gustav refuses to take it and sell the home, claiming he is not obligated to perform on their agreement because the Statute of Frauds requires the sale of real property be made in writing. What can Frank show that would require Gustav to go through with the oral agreement to sell?

A. That Gustav would be unjustly enriched if he did not sell.

B. That Fiona's actions equal partial performance on the agreement, requiring Gustav to sell.

C. That Frank relied on Gustav's promise to his detriment.

D. That Fiona has established adverse possession.

Question 2

Diana and John own commercial buildings next to each other in an industrial section of town. Diana bought the property and uses it as a storage facility for products that she sells in her store front downtown; she rarely if ever goes there. John uses his building as a manufacturing center for his products and goes to the building every day. John decides he needs more room for trucks to park next to his building and widens its driveway encroaching on Diana's property by 2 feet. Diana doesn't notice because she is not at her building and doesn't come back for 4 years. Diana and John's state has a statutory possession time frame of 3 years. What real property theory gives John the right to now own the 2 feet of Diana's property on which his driveway extends?

- **A.** Easement
- **B.** Leasehold
- **C.** Covenant
- **D.** Adverse Possession

Question 3

Cameron and Maya were dating and living together in an apartment. They decided to buy a home together and did so as tenants in common. Maya soon became pregnant and had a daughter named Trisha. Cameron and Maya then got married. However, they disagreed on how Trisha should be raised and their constant arguing led to divorce. Maya and Trisha remained living in the house, while Cameron left town. He then conveyed the title and interest in the house to his daughter. Soon after, he was in an auto accident and died without a will. Who now owns the house?

- **A.** Maya and Cameron's heirs
- **B.** Maya
- **C.** Maya and Trisha
- **D.** Trisha

Question 4

High Power, Inc., the local utility company, established underground pipelines in a 50 acre area to serve as gas transportation lines to future homes. Soon after, subdivisions are built over the pipelines, and the homes purchased with an easement remaining in the interest of High Power for the pipes. One subdivision does not succeed, and no homes are purchased there. The subdivision builder goes bankrupt and leaves the homes abandoned. The pipelines under those homes are never turned on or used. After 20 years, a new builder wants to buy the unsuccessful subdivision, tear down the houses, and build a commercial water park. What would allow the new builder to purchase the land without the pipeline easement?

- **A.** The Statute of Limitations
- **B.** Abandonment of the easement by High Power

C. Adverse Possession

D. Quitclaim Deed

Question 5

Deliah wants to buy a house, and finds one that she falls in love with. She works as a real property title examiner in her county. She offers the owner twice the amount he is asking for and he accepts. However, he had already sold the house to Eliza 1 month before, but she was not moving into the house for another month and the owner left the For Sale sign in his yard. What should Deliah have had that will prevent her from purchasing the house?

A. Constructive Notice

B. Actual Notice

C. Acquired Title

D. Necessity

Tort Law Outline: Overview

Approximately half of the Torts questions for each MBE will be based on category II, and approximately half will be based on the remaining categories, I, III, IV, and V. All of the major topics (designated by Roman numerals) will be represented in each examination, but not necessarily all of the subtopics.

Note: The Torts questions should be answered according to principles of general applicability. Examinees are to assume that there is no applicable statute unless otherwise specified; however, survival actions and claims for wrongful death should be assumed to be available where applicable. Examinees should assume that joint and several liability, with pure comparative negligence, is the relevant rule unless otherwise indicated.

I. **INTENTIONAL TORTS**
   A. Harms to the person: assault, battery, false imprisonment, infliction of mental distress
   B. Harms to property interests; trespass to land and chattels, conversion
   C. Defenses to claims for physical harms
      1. Consent
      2. Privileges and immunities: protection of self and others; protection of property interests; parental discipline; protection of public interests; necessity; incomplete privilege

II. **NEGLIGENCE**
   A. The duty question: including failure to act; unforeseeable plaintiffs; and obligations to control the conduct of third parties
   B. The standard of care
      1. The reasonably prudent person: including children, physically and mentally impaired individuals, professional people, and other special classes
      2. Rules of conduct derived from statutes and custom
   C. Problems relating to proof of fault, including res ipsa loquitur

D. Problems relating to causation
   1. But for and substantial causes
   2. Harms traceable to multiple causes
   3. Questions of apportionment of responsibility among multiple tortfeasors, including joint and several liability
E. Limitations on liability and special rules of liability
   1. Problems relating to "remote" or "unforeseeable" causes, "legal" or "proximate" cause, and "superseding" causes
   2. Claims against owners and occupiers of land
   3. Claims for mental distress not arising from physical harm; other intangible injuries
   4. Claims for pure economic loss
F. Liability for acts of others
   1. Employees and other agents
   2. Independent contractors and nondelegable duties
G. Defenses
   1. Contributory fault: including common law contributory negligence and last clear chance, and the various forms of comparative negligence
   2. Assumption of risk

III. STRICT LIABILITY: CLAIMS ARISING FROM ABNORMALLY DANGEROUS ACTIVITIES; THE RULE OF *RYLANDS V. FLETCHER* AND OTHER COMMON LAW STRICT LIABILITY CLAIMS; DEFENSES

IV. PRODUCTS LIABILITY: CLAIMS AGAINST MANUFACTURERS AND OTHERS BASED ON DEFECTS IN MANUFACTURE, DESIGN, AND WARNING; AND DEFENSES

V. OTHER TORTS
A. Claims based on nuisance, and defenses
B. Claims based on defamation and invasion of privacy; defenses and constitutional limitations
C. Claims based on misrepresentations, and defenses
D. Claims based on intentional interference with business relations, and defenses

⚭ Key Focus Areas for Tort Law

Negligence and other torts

Introduction to Tort Law

The starting point in the analysis of torts questions always has to be: "What is the theory of this case? Is this case an intentional tort theory? Is it negligence? Is it strict liability?" Always do the analysis to get to the "right" answer. After reading the question, make a notation in the margin as to the theory of the case before reading the answer choices. This will force you to think through the theory before evaluating the possible answers.

Remember that in torts, there can be multiple tortfeasors. Do not get caught up in the causation issue, which was important in law school but does not lend itself to multiple choice testing. Often questions will include a victim, and two others who have done something wrong. Do not assume that a person who has acted wrongly in response to another's wrongdoing is not accountable for his or her actions. Usually, both parties will be held accountable for what they have done.

Approaching Tort Law Using IRAC

Lloyd and Benson were old friends who enjoyed hunting together. One weekend Lloyd and Benson went on a quail hunting expedition in a remote wilderness area deep in the Wasatch Mountains of northeastern Utah. They were hunting in a very desolate area surrounded by mountainous terrain located at least fifty miles from any habitation. With hunting rifles in hand they were ambling around, but no game was visible. After a rather uneventful morning with nothing to shoot at, Lloyd suddenly spotted a Utah condor, a large nearly extinct vulture. The condor was of an endangered species and to shoot one in Utah was a criminal offense.

Unable to resist the temptation, Lloyd took a shot at the condor. The bullet missed the vulture but struck Bush, a state forest ranger, who was hiding in a secluded area watching a trail frequented by drug smugglers. The bullet hit Bush in the eye and permanently blinded him. Neither Lloyd nor Benson were aware of Bush's presence.

If Bush asserts a claim against Lloyd to recover damages for his injury, Bush will:

A. Prevail, if Lloyd negligently shot the gun.

B. Prevail, because Lloyd intended to shoot the condor.

C. Not prevail, because Lloyd had no reason to anticipate the presence of another person in such a remote area.

D. Not prevail, if the bullet ricocheted off a tree and hit Bush.

IRAC Answer

Issue: Whether or not Bush is a foreseeable plaintiff owed a duty of care by Lloyd the defendant.

Rule: In order to be liable for negligence, the defendant's conduct must constitute the legal or proximate cause of plaintiff's harm or injury. According to the rule enunciated in the Palsgraf case, Judge Cardozo stated that a defendant's duty of care is owed only to foreseeable plaintiffs (i.e., those individuals who are within the risk of harm created by defendant's unreasonable conduct).

Application: Bush is an unforeseeable plaintiff to whom no duty of care is owed.

Conclusion: "C" Lloyd had no reason to anticipate the presence of another person in such a remote area.

Questions 1-3 Are Based on the Following

Two sisters, Darla and Irene, are in business together selling natural cosmetics. They hand pick the herbs, plants, and flowers that will go into their products and know growers who have become their regular customers. Irene contacts James, a flower grower, to buy more flowers. But, Irene learns from James's wife that James is not around because his farm and shop have been robbed, and there are broken and crushed flowers laying all over his open shop and farmland. Irene convinces her nephew to go to James's place while James and his wife are at the police station, and take some of the crushed and broken flowers, which Irene says, "James will never miss." The nephew brings back 10 pounds of flowers. Darla learns what her sister has done, is outraged, and refuses to do business with Irene anymore.

Question 1

If Irene campaigning to be the mayor of her town, and wins, and Darla writes a letter to the editor of the town newspaper disclosing Irene's business misconduct, would Darla have any defenses to Irene's defamation lawsuit against her?

- **A.** No, because Darla made Irene's misconduct public knowledge without Irene's consent.

- **B.** No, because the public had no need to know of Irene's misconduct.

- **C.** Yes, because Darla's statement is the truth.

- **D.** Yes, because Darla's statement is the truth and was written without malice.

Question 2

When Irene accepts the flowers that her nephew has taken from James's store and farm but does not pay James for them, what tort has she committed?

- **A.** Trespass to Real Property

- **B.** Trespass to Personal Property

- **C.** Conversion

- **D.** Disparagement

Question 3

Irene, angry at her sister, writes a letter to their town newspaper falsely accusing Darla of having sexual relations with their minor nephew. What tort should Darla sue Irene for?

- **A.** Slander

- **B.** Libel

- **C.** Slander Per Se

- **D.** Libel Per Se

New Hampshire has a state statute prohibiting a person who participates in the sport of skiing from suing a ski resort operator for injuries caused by the risks inherent in skiing. Alaina goes to a New Hampshire ski resort to go snow tubing. She snow tubes down a snow tube run, designed exclusively for tubing. No resort employees monitored this run. On her fourth run down, Alaina crossed the center line between runs and collided with another snow tuber and was injured. She sued the ski resort for her injuries.

Question 4

What defense with the ski resort assert in Alaina's lawsuit against them?

    A. Negligence Per Se

    B. Assumption of the Risk

    C. Danger Invites Rescue

    D. Contributory Negligence

Question 5

Alaina's lawsuit against the ski resort goes to a jury trial, and the jury says that Alaina is partly at fault for the accident. Under what doctrine might her damages be reduced in proportion to the degree to which she was negligent?

    A. Comparative Negligence

    B. Contributory Negligence

    C. Assumption of the Risk

    D. Strict Liability

Question 6

Stanley is a very cautious man, who tries to take extra care in making sure his actions do not harm others. Stanley buys a large trampoline for his grandchildren to play on when they visit him twice a year. At other times of the year, the trampoline remains in the middle of his unfenced backyard. William, a nine-year-old neighbor of Stanley's, sees the trampoline and runs into Stanley's backyard to play on it. Stanley is not at home at the time. William bounces for five minutes, then slips and twists his ankle. William calls for help, but no one hears, so William has to crawl home, further injuring his ankle. William's mother sues Stanley for William's injuries. What tort action might be most successful for William's mother?

    A. Trespass to land

    B. Trespass to property

    C. Attractive Nuisance

    D. Neglect

Question 7

Chen graduates from college with an accounting degree, and the highest GPA in his major. He passes the CPA exam with flying colors and is offered many accounting jobs. Chen decides to work for MolaRola, a very large soda beverage manufacturer, and signs an employment agreement with them. Bebsi, another very large soda beverage manufacturer who does not know that Chen has already signed another agreement, then offers Chen a higher paying, better benefit job at their company. Chen breaches his employment agreement with MolaRola and goes to work for Bebsi. MolaRola finds out that Bebsi has hired their prize accountant and sues Bebsi. What tort action would be successful for MolaRola in suing Bebsi?

A. Wrongful Interference with a Contractual Relationship

B. Wrongful Interference with a Business Relationship

C. Fraud

D. None of the above

Question 8

Becky goes to Diamond Dave's Used Cars to buy a car. Diamond Dave starts telling Becky about all the wonderful features of a 3-year-old Chevy Suburban on the lot. Diamond Dave claims it is the fastest car on the lot, it has wonderful fuel efficiency, and it won't need an oil change for at least 15,000 miles. Becky is very excited by Diamond Dave's statements and buys the Suburban on the spot. However, it is a slow car that uses a lot of gas and needs oil changes every 7,000 miles. Becky sues Diamond Dave for fraud. Will Becky's suit be successful?

A. Yes, because Dave lied about the car.

B. Yes, because Becky was an innocent party.

C. No, because Dave is a salesman giving his opinion.

D. No, because Dave did not cause injury to Becky.

Questions 9-10 Are Based on the Following

Trevor wants a new pet, but he wants something unique that will make him popular among his peers. Trevor decides to buy a Bengal Tiger. He keeps the tiger in a sheltered cage in his backyard, and lets it out to go on leashed walks with him around the neighborhood. Trevor becomes very popular at work, and his coworker, Roni, asks if he can borrow the tiger for his upcoming jungle theme party. Trevor agrees to lend out the tiger, even though he was not invited to the party. At the party, the caged tiger is a very popular attraction and one partygoer, Mona, starts to tease the tiger with her beef skewer appetizer. The tiger, which has not been fed, lunges for the appetizer, breaking the cage and injuring Mona.

Question 9

If Mona sues Roni in intentional tort for her injuries, will she succeed?

A. No, because it was her fault for teasing the tiger.

B. No, because Roni was not the owner of the tiger.

C. Yes, because Roni forgot to feed the tiger while it was in his care.

D. Yes, because Roni failed to warn of the tiger's danger.

Question 10

If Mona sues Trevor in intentional tort for her injuries, will she succeed?

    A. No, because Trevor was not at the party.

    B. No, because the tiger was in Roni's care at the time of the injury.

    C. Yes, because Trevor is the wild animal's owner.

    D. Yes, because the tiger is rabid.

Business Ethics: Making the Decisions

People make decisions every day in business. Some results are positive, while others are harmful. The act of making the decision may be identified as ethical or unethical. The ethical standards that govern the behavior are higher standards than the law—they are the generally accepted rules of conduct that govern society, the unwritten rules for behavior expectations

Philosophers have debated the dilemma of ethics for centuries, developing definitions from their own points of view. Many theories of ethics have evolved providing tools to assist in the analysis of ethical dilemmas. The following well-known theories (and theorists) are used in making ethical business decisions.

Divine Command Theory

Applying this theory, individuals resolve dilemmas based on religious beliefs. We can see this theory influencing the law, for instance, in Muslim nations where adultery is illegal because it is unethical based on Muslim belief. The theory also applies to natural law, which the Creator has given, such as human rights identified in the U.S. Declaration of Independence.

Ethical Egoism Theory

In this theory, actions are grounded in self-interest. Without laws to control self-interest and protect individuals, chaos abounds.

Theorists: Thomas Hobbes and Adam Smith

Utilitarian Theory

The greatest good for the greatest number is the decision tool used in applying this theory. Some are disgruntled, but it addresses the critical mass. Historically, philosophers have applied this theory to healthcare, electricity, cars and outsourcing to developing countries.

Theorists: Jeremy Bentham and John Stuart Mill

SOURCE: Jennings, M.M. (2009). *Business ethics: Case Studies and selected readings.* Mason, OH, South Western.

Categorical Imperative

Applying this theory requires that one does not use others in such a way as to obtain a one-sided benefit. The principle is to act only in a way that one would find comfortable if it became a universal law. The outcome must be fair and the decision made for the right reason.

Theorists: Immanuel Kant

The Contractarians and Justice

A social contract is the way to think about this theory. The guiding principle is that rational people will choose the most equitable and fairest result.

Theorists: John Locke and John Rawls

Rights Theory

In this theory everyone has a set of rights and the government is in place to protect those rights. Some dilemmas where philosophers apply this theory include abortion, slavery, property, justice, animal rights, privacy and euthanasia.

Theorists: Robert Nozick

Moral Relativists

This theory dictates that circumstance rules decisions. There are no absolutes. The pressure of the moment determines whether the action taken is justified.

Virtue Ethics

For Plato and Aristotle, resolving ethical dilemmas required developing virtue. Developing these virtues took place through training and knowledge acquisition. According to this theory, business decisions involve the application of one or more of the following virtues:

> Ability, Acceptance, Amiability, Articulateness, Attentiveness, Autonomy, Caring, Charisma, Compassion, Cool-headedness, Courage, Determination, Fairness, Generosity, Graciousness, Gratitude, Heroism, Honesty, Humility, Humor, Independence, Integrity, Justice, Loyalty, Pride, Prudence, Responsibility, Saintliness, Shame (capable of), Spirit, Toughness, Trust, Trustworthiness, Wittiness, and Zeal.

Theorist: Robert Solomon

Many models for solving ethical dilemmas emerge from the field of ethics. Some of the models applied to business include those of Dr. Peter Drucker, management expert; Laura Nash, Harvard Divinity School; Ken Blanchard and Dr. Norman Vincent Peale, people experts and authors; and Warren Buffet, investor and philanthropist.

Drucker's test is simple: "Above all do no harm." Intentionally making decisions that will not do harm will encourage ethical decision-making. Likewise, Buffet's simple front-page-of-the-paper test supports critical thinking to envision how the decision may look on the front page of a paper before making the final decision. Blanchard and Peale subscribe to a three- question test: "Is it legal?" "Is it balanced?" and "How does it make me feel?" This method considers the law, society and the individual's conscience. Finally, Laura Nash's comprehensive model allows for the incorporation of perspective, alternative views and historical consideration in the decision making process. Her twelve questions are:

1. Have you defined the problem accurately?

2. How would you define the problem if you stood on the other side of the fence?

3. How did this situation occur in the first place?

4. To whom and what do you give your loyalties as a person and as a member of the corporation?

5. What is your intention in making this decision?

6. How does this intention compare with the likely results?

7. Whom could your decision or action injure?

8. Can you engage the affected parties in the discussion of the problem before you make your decision?

9. Are you confident that your position will be as valid over a long period of time as it seems now?

10. Could you disclose without qualms your decision or action to your boss, your CEO, the board of directors, your family or society as a whole?

11. What is the symbolic potential of your action if understood? If misunderstood?

12. Under what conditions would you allow exceptions to your stand?

Ethical decision making is part of business. The intention of this section is to show that there is no one right theory or model; instead there are many tools available to assist in making business decisions.

Georgia Rules of Professional Conduct

Part IV (After January 1, 2001)— Georgia Rules of Professional Conduct

SOURCE: Georgia Supreme Court.

For more details visit:
www.gabar.org/barrules/ethics and professionalism/index.cfm

Georgia Code of Judicial Conduct

⌾ **Preamble**

Our legal system is based on the principle that an independent, fair, and competent judiciary will interpret and apply the laws that govern us. The role of the judiciary is central to American concepts of justice and the rule of law. Intrinsic to all sections of this Code are the precepts that judges, individually and collectively, must respect and honor the judicial office as a public trust and strive to enhance and maintain confidence in our legal system.

Every judge should strive to maintain the dignity appropriate to the judicial office. The judge is an arbiter of facts and law for the resolution of disputes and a highly visible symbol of government under the rule of law. As a result, judges should be held to a higher standard, and should aspire to conduct themselves with the dignity accorded their esteemed position.

The Code of Judicial Conduct is intended to establish standards for the ethical conduct of judges. It consists of broad statements called Canons, specific rules set forth in Sections under each Canon, a Terminology Section, an Application Section, and Commentary. The text of the Canons and the Sections, including the Terminology and Application Sections, is authoritative. The Commentary, by explanation and example, provides guidance with respect to the purpose and meaning of the Canons and Sections. The Commentary is not intended as a statement of additional rules. When the text uses "shall" or "shall not," it is intended to impose binding obligations, the violation of which can result in disciplinary action. When "should" or "should not" is used, the text is intended as advisory and as a statement of what is or is not appropriate conduct, but not as a binding rule under which a judge may be disciplined. When "may" is used, it denotes permissible discretion or, depending on the context, it refers to action that is not covered by specific proscriptions.

The Canons and Sections are rules of reason. They should be applied consistent with constitutional requirements, statutes, other court rules and decisional law, as well as in the context of all relevant circumstances. The Code is to be construed so as not to impinge on the essential independence of judges in making judicial decisions, or on judges' First Amendment rights of freedom of speech and association.

The Code is designed to provide guidance to judges and candidates for judicial office and to provide a structure for regulating conduct through disciplinary agencies. It is not designed for nor intended as a basis for civil liability or criminal prosecution. Furthermore, the purpose of the Code would be subverted if the Code were invoked by lawyers for mere tactical advantage in a proceeding.

The text of the Canons and Sections is intended to govern conduct of judges and to be binding upon them. It is not intended, however, that every transgression will result in disciplinary action. Whether disciplinary action is appropriate, and the degree of discipline to be imposed, should be determined through a reasonable and reasoned application of the text and should depend on such factors as the seriousness of the transgression, whether there is a pattern of improper activity, and the effect of the improper activity on others or on the judicial system. The Code of Judicial Conduct is not intended as an exhaustive guide for the conduct of judges. They should also be governed in their judicial and personal conduct by general ethical standards. The mandatory provisions of the Canons and Sections describe the basic minimal ethical requirements of judicial conduct. Judges and candidates should strive to achieve the highest ethical standards, even if not required by this Code. As an example, a judge or candidate is permitted under Canon 7, Section B, to solicit campaign funds directly from potential donors. The Commentary, however, makes clear that the judge or candidate who wishes to exceed the minimal ethical requirements would choose to set up a campaign committee to raise and solicit contributions. The Code is intended to state only basic standards which should govern the conduct of all judges and to provide guidance to assist judges in establishing and maintaining high standards of judicial and personal conduct.

Terms explained below are noted with an asterisk (*) in the Sections where they appear. In addition, the Sections where terms appear are referred to after the explanation of each term below.

"Appropriate Authority" denotes the authority with responsibility for initiation of disciplinary process with respect to the violation to be reported. See Sections 3D(1) and 3D(2).

"Candidate." A candidate is a person seeking selection for or retention in judicial office by election or appointment. A person becomes a candidate for judicial office as soon as he or she appoints and/or forms a campaign committee, makes a public announcement of candidacy, declares or files as a candidate with the election or appointment authority, or authorizes solicitation or acceptance of contributions or support. The term "candidate" has the same meaning when applied to a judge seeking election or appointment to non-judicial office. See Preamble and Sections 7A(1), 7A(2), 7B(1), 7B(2), and 7C.

"Comment" in connection with a case refers to valuative statements judging the professional wisdom of specific lawyering tactics or the legal correctness of particular court decisions. In contrast, it does not mean the giving of generally informative explanations to describe litigation factors including the prima facie legal elements of case types pending before the courts, legal concepts such as burden of proof and duty of persuasion or principles such as innocent until proven guilty and knowing waiver of constitutional rights, variable realities illustrated by hypothetical factual patterns of aggravating or mitigating conduct, procedural phases of unfolding lawsuits, the social policy goals behind the law subject to application in various cases, as well as competing theories about what the law should be. See Section 3B(9).

"Court personnel" does not include the lawyers in a proceeding before a judge. See Sections 3B(7)(c) and 3B(9).

"De minimis" denotes an insignificant interest that could not raise reasonable question as to a judge's impartiality. See Section 3E(1)(c).

"**Economic interest**" denotes ownership of a more than de minimis legal or equitable interest, or a relationship as officer, director, advisor, or other active participant in the affairs of a party, except that:

(i) ownership of an interest in a mutual or common investment fund that holds securities is not an economic interest in such securities unless the judge participates in the management of the fund or a proceeding pending or impending before the judge could substantially affect the value of the interest;

(ii) service by a judge as an officer, director, advisor, or other active participant in an educational, religious, charitable, fraternal, or civic organization, or service by a judge's spouse, parent, or child as an officer, director, advisor, or other active participant in any organization does not create an economic interest in securities held by that organization;

(iii) a deposit in a financial institution, the proprietary interest of a policy holder in a mutual insurance company, of a depositor in a mutual savings association, is not an economic interest in the organization unless a proceeding pending or impending before the judge could substantially affect the value of the interest;

(iv) ownership of government securities is not an economic interest in the issuer unless a proceeding pending or impending before the judge could substantially affect the value of the securities. See Section 3E(2).

"**Fiduciary**" includes such relationships as executor, administrator, trustee, and guardian. See Sections 3E(2) and 5D.

"**Invidious discrimination**" is any action by an organization that characterizes some immutable individual trait such as a person's race, gender, or national origin, as well as religion, as odious or as signifying inferiority, which therefore is used to justify arbitrary exclusion of persons possessing those traits from membership, position, or participation in the organization. See Section 2C.

"**Knowingly**," "**knowledge**," "**known**," or "**knows**" denotes actual knowledge of the fact in question. A person's knowledge may be inferred from circumstances. See Sections 3D(1), 3D(2), and 3E(1).

"**Law**" denotes court rules as well as statutes, constitutional provisions, and decisional law. See Sections 2A, 3A, 3B(2), 3B(7), 4A, 4B, 4C, 5C(4), 5F, and 5G.

"**Member of the judge's family residing in the judge's household**" denotes any relative of the judge by blood or marriage, or a person treated by a judge as a member of the judge's family, who resided in the judge's household. See Sections 3E(1)(c) and 5C(4).

"**Non-public information**" denotes information that, by law, is not available to the public. Non-public information may include but is not limited to: information that is sealed by statute or court order, impounded or communicated in camera; and information offered in grand jury proceedings, pre-sentencing reports, dependency cases, or psychiatric reports. See Section 3B(11).

"**Political organization**" denotes a political party or other group, the principal purpose of which is to further the election or appointment of candidates to political office. See Section 7A(1).

"**Public election.**" This term includes primary and general elections; it includes partisan elections, nonpartisan elections, and may include (as context demands) retention elections. See Sections 7A(1), 7A(2), 7B(1), and 7B(2).

"Require." The rules prescribing that a judge "require" certain conduct of others are, like all of the rules in this Code, rules of reason. The use of the term "require" in that context means a judge is to exercise reasonable direction and control over the conduct of those persons subject to the judge's direction and control. See Sections 3B(3), 3B(4), 3B(6), 3B(9), and 3C(2).

"Third degree of relationship." The following persons are relatives within the third degree of relationship: great-grandparent, grandparent, parent, uncle, aunt, brother, sister, child, grandchild, great-grandchild, nephew, or niece. See Section 3E(1)(c).

∞ Canon 1

Judges Shall Uphold the Integrity and Independence of the Judiciary.

An independent and honorable judiciary is indispensable to justice in our society. Judges shall participate in establishing, maintaining, and enforcing high standards of conduct, and shall personally observe such standards of conduct so that the integrity and independence of the judiciary may be preserved. The provisions of this Code should be construed and applied to further that objective.

Commentary: Deference to the judgments and rulings of courts depends upon public confidence in the integrity and independence of judges. The integrity and independence of judges depends in turn upon their acting without fear or favor. Although judges should be independent, they must comply with the law, including the provisions of this Code. Public confidence in the impartiality of the judiciary is maintained by the adherence of each judge to this responsibility. Conversely, violation of this Code diminishes public confidence in the judiciary and thereby does injury to the system of government under law.

∞ Canon 2

Judges Shall Avoid Impropriety and the Appearance of Impropriety in All Their Activities.

A. Judges shall respect and comply with the law* and shall act at all times in a manner that promotes public confidence in the integrity and impartiality of the judiciary.

Commentary: Public confidence in the judiciary is eroded by irresponsible or improper conduct of judges. Judges must avoid all impropriety and appearance of impropriety. Judges must expect to be the subject of constant public scrutiny. Judges must therefore accept restrictions on their conduct that might be viewed as burdensome by the ordinary citizen, and they should do so freely and willingly. The prohibition against behaving with impropriety or the appearance of impropriety applies to both the professional and personal conduct of a judge. Because it is not practicable to list all prohibited acts, the proscription is necessarily cast in general terms that extend to conduct by judges that is harmful although not specifically mentioned in the Code. Actual improprieties under this standard include violations of law, court rules, or other specific provisions of this Code. The test for appearance of impropriety is whether the conduct would create in reasonable minds a perception that the judge's ability to carry out judicial responsibilities with integrity, impartiality and competence is impaired. See also, Commentary under Section 2C.

B. Judges shall not allow their family, social, political, or other relationships to influence their judicial conduct or judgment. Judges shall not lend the prestige of judicial office to advance the private interests of the judge or others; nor should they convey or permit others to convey the impression that they are in a special position to influence them. Judges should not testify voluntarily as character witnesses.

Commentary: Maintaining the prestige of judicial office is essential to a system of government in which the judiciary functions independently of the executive and legislative branches. Respect for the judicial office facilitates the orderly conduct of legitimate judicial functions. Judges should distinguish between proper and improper use of the prestige of office in all of their activities. For example, it would be improper for a judge to allude to his or her judgeship to gain a personal advantage such as deferential treatment when stopped by a police officer for a traffic offense. Similarly, judicial letterhead must not be used for conducting a judge's personal business.

A judge must avoid lending the prestige of judicial office for the advancement of the private interests of others. For example, a judge must not use the judge's position to gain advantage in a civil suit involving a member of the judge's family. In contracts for publication of a judge's writings, a judge should retain control over the a.dvertising to avoid exploitation of the judge's office. As to the acceptance of awards. See Section 5C (4)(a) and Commentary. Although a judge should be sensitive to possible abuse of the prestige of office, a judge may, based on the judge's personal knowledge, serve as a reference or provide a letter of recommendation. However, a judge must not initiate the communication of information to a sentencing judge or probation or corrections officer, but may provide to such person information for the record in response to a formal request.

Judges may participate in the process of judicial selection by cooperating with appointing authorities and screening committees seeking names for consideration, and by responding to official inquiries concerning a person being considered for a judgeship. See also Canon 7, regarding use of a judge's name in political activities. A judge must not testify voluntarily as a character witness, because to do so may lend the prestige of the judicial office in support of a party for whom the judge testifies. Moreover, when a judge testifies as a witness, a lawyer who regularly appears before the judge may be placed in the awkward position of cross-examining the judge. A judge may, however, testify when properly summoned. Except in unusual circumstances where the demands of justice require, a judge should discourage a party from requiring the judge to testify as a character witness.

C. Judges shall not hold membership in any organization that practices invidious discrimination.*

Commentary: Membership by a judge in an organization that practices invidious discrimination may give rise to perceptions that the judge's impartiality is impaired. Section 2C refers to the current practices of the organization. Whether an organization practices invidious discrimination is often a complex question to which judges should be sensitive. The answer cannot be determined from a mere examination of an organization's current membership rolls, but rather depends on how the organization selects members and other relevant factors, such as whether the organization is dedicated to the preservation of religious, ethnic, or cultural values of legitimate common interest to its members, or whether it is in fact and effect an intimate, purely private organization whose membership limitations could not be constitutionally prohibited. Absent such factors, an organization is generally said to discriminate invidiously if it arbitrarily excludes from membership on the basis of race, religion, sex, or national origin persons who would otherwise be admitted to membership. See New York State Club Ass'n. Inc. v. City of New York, 108 S. Ct. 2225, 101 L.Ed.2d1 (1988); Board of Directors of Rotary International v. Rotary Club of Duarte, 481 U. S. 537, 107 S. Ct. 1940, 95 L. Ed. 2d. 474 (1987); Roberts v. United State Jaycees, 468 U. S. 609, 104 S. Ct. 3244, 82 L.Ed.2d.462 (1984). Ultimately, each judge must determine in the judge's own conscience whether an organization of which the judge is a member practices invidious discrimination.

⌒⌒ Canon 3

Judges Shall Perform the Duties of Their Office Impartially and Diligently.

A. Judicial Duties in General.

The judicial duties of judges take precedence over all their other activities. Their judicial duties include all the duties of their offices prescribed by law.* In the performance of these duties, the following standards apply:

B. Adjudicative Responsibilities.

(1) Judges shall hear and decide matters assigned to them, except those in which they are disqualified.

(2) Judges should be faithful to the law* and maintain professional competence in it. Judges shall not be swayed by partisan interests, public clamor, or fear of criticism.

(3) Judges shall require* order and decorum in proceedings over which they preside.

(4) Judges shall be patient, dignified, and courteous to litigants, jurors, witnesses, lawyers, and others with whom they deal in their official capacity, and shall require* similar conduct of lawyers, and of staffs, court officials, and others subject to their direction and control.

Commentary: The duty to hear all proceedings fairly and with patience is not inconsistent with the duty to dispose promptly of the business of the court. Judges can be efficient and business-like while being patient and deliberate.

(5) Judges shall perform judicial duties without bias or prejudice. Judges shall not, in the performance of judicial duties, by words or conduct manifest bias or prejudice, including but not limited to bias or prejudice based upon race, sex, religion, national origin, disability, age, sexual orientation, or socio-economic status, and shall not permit staff, court officials, and others subject to judicial direction and control to do so.

Commentary: Judges must refrain from speech, gestures, or other conduct that could reasonably be perceived as sexual harassment and must require the same standard of conduct of others subject to their direction and control. Judges must perform judicial duties impartially and fairly. Judges who manifest bias on any basis in a proceeding impair the fairness of the proceeding and bring the judiciary into disrepute. Facial expression, body language, in addition to oral communication, can give to parties or lawyers in the proceeding, jurors, the media, and others an appearance of judicial bias. Judges must be alert to avoid behavior that may be perceived as prejudicial.

(6) Judges shall require* lawyers in proceedings before the court to refrain from manifesting, by words and conduct, bias or prejudice based upon race, sex, religion, national origin, disability, age, sexual orientation, or socio-economic status, against parties, witnesses, counsel or others. This Section, 3B(6), does not preclude legitimate advocacy when race, sex, religion, national origin, disability, age, sexual orientation, or socio-economic status, or other similar factors, are issues in the proceeding.

(7) Judges shall accord to every person who has a legal interest in a proceeding, or that person's lawyer, the right to be heard according to law.* Judges shall not initiate or consider ex parte communications, or consider other communications made to them

outside the presence of the parties concerning a pending or impending proceeding, except that:

(a) where circumstances require, ex parte communications for scheduling, where administrative purposes or emergencies that do not deal with substantive matters or issues on the merits are authorized; provided:

    (i) the judge reasonably believes that no party will gain a procedural or tactical advantage as a result of the ex parte communication, and

    (ii) the judge makes provision promptly to notify all other parties of the substance of the ex parte communication and allows an opportunity to respond.

(b) Judges may obtain the advice of a disinterested expert on the law* applicable to a proceeding before the court, if they give notice to the parties of the person consulted and the substance of the advice, and afford the parties reasonable opportunity to respond.

(c) Judges may consult with court personnel* whose function is to aid them in carrying out their adjudicative responsibilities, or with other judges.

(d) Judges may, with the consent of the parties, confer separately with the parties or their lawyers in an effort to mediate or settle matters before the court.

(e) Judges may initiate or consider any ex parte communications when expressly authorized by law* to do so.

Commentary: The proscription against communications concerning a proceeding includes communications from lawyers, law teachers, and other persons who are not participants in the proceeding, except to the limited extent permitted. To the extent reasonably possible, all parties or their lawyers shall be included in communications with a judge. Whenever presence of a party or notice to a party is required by Section 3B(7), it is the party's lawyer, or if the party is unrepresented, the party, who is to be present or to whom notice is given. An appropriate and often desirable procedure for a court to obtain the advice of a disinterested expert on legal issues is to invite the expert to file a brief amicus curiae. Certain ex parte communication is approved by Section 3B(7) to facilitate scheduling and other administrative purposes and to accommodate emergencies. In general, however, judges must discourage ex parte communication and allow it only if all the criteria stated in Section 3B(7) are clearly met. Judges must disclose to all parties all ex parte communications described in Section 3B(7)(a) and 3B(7)(b) regarding a proceeding pending or impending before them. Judges must not independently investigate facts in a case and must consider only the evidence presented. Judges may request a party to submit proposed findings of fact and conclusions of law, so long as the other parties are apprised of the request and are given an opportunity to respond to the proposed findings and conclusions. Judges must take reasonable efforts, including the provision of appropriate supervision, to ensure that Section 3B(7) is not violated through law clerks or other personnel on their staff. If communication between the trial judge and the appellate court with respect to a proceeding is permitted, a copy of any written communication or the substance of any oral communication should be provided to all parties.

(8) Judges shall dispose of all judicial matters fairly, promptly, and efficiently.

Commentary: In disposing of matters promptly, efficiently and fairly, judges must demonstrate due regard for the rights of the parties to be heard and to have issues resolved without unnecessary cost or delay. Containing costs while preserving fundamental rights of parties also protects the interests of witnesses and the general public. Judges should monitor and supervise cases so as to reduce or eliminate dilatory practices, avoidable delays, and unnecessary costs. Judges should encourage and seek to facilitate settlement, but parties should not feel coerced into surrendering the right to have their controversy resolved by courts.

> (a) The obligation of a judge to dispose of matters promptly and efficiently must not take precedence over the judge's obligation to dispose of matters fairly and with patience.

Commentary: Prompt disposition of the court's business requires judges to devote adequate time to their duties, to be punctual in attending court and expeditious in determining matters under submission, and to insist that court officials, litigants, and their lawyers cooperate with them to that end.

> (9) Judges shall not, while a proceeding is pending or impending in any court, make any public comment* that might reasonably be expected to affect its outcome or impair its fairness, or make any non-public comment that might substantially interfere with a fair trial or hearing. Judges shall require* similar abstention on the part of court personnel* subject to their direction and control. This subsection does not prohibit judges from making public statements in the course of their official duties or from explaining for public information the procedures of the court. This Section does not apply to proceedings in which the judge is a litigant in a personal capacity.

Commentary: The requirement that judges abstain from public comment regarding a pending or impending proceeding continues during any appellate process and until final disposition. This Section does not prohibit judges from commenting on proceedings in which the judge is a litigant in a personal capacity, but in cases such as a writ of mandamus where a judge is a litigant in an official capacity, the judge must not comment publicly.

> (10) Judges shall not commend or criticize jurors for their verdict other than in a court order or opinion in a proceeding, but may express appreciation to jurors for their service to the judicial system and the community.

Commentary: Commending or criticizing jurors for their verdict may imply a judicial expectation in future cases and may impair a juror's ability to be fair and impartial.

> (11) Judges shall not disclose or use, for any purpose unrelated to judicial duties, non-public information* acquired in a judicial capacity.

C. Administrative Responsibilities

> (1) Judges shall diligently discharge their administrative responsibilities without bias or prejudice, maintain professional competence in judicial administration, and should cooperate with other judges and court officials in the administration of court business.
> (2) Judges shall require* their staffs, court officials and others subject to their direction and control to observe the standards of fidelity and diligence that apply to the judges and to refrain from manifesting bias or prejudice in the performance of their official duties.

(3) Judges with supervisory authority for judicial performance of other judges should take reasonable measures to assure the prompt disposition of matters before them and the proper performance of their other judicial responsibilities.

(4) Judges shall not make unnecessary appointments. Judges shall exercise the power of appointment impartially and on the basis of merit. Judges shall avoid nepotism and favoritism. Judges shall not approve compensation of appointees beyond the fair value of services rendered.

Commentary: Appointees of judges include assigned counsel, officials such as referees, commissioners, special masters, receivers, guardians, and personnel such as clerks, secretaries, and bailiffs. Consent by the parties to an appointment or an award of compensation does not relieve the judge of the obligation prescribed by Section 3C(4).

D. Disciplinary Responsibilities

(1) Judges who receive information indicating a substantial likelihood that another judge has committed a violation of this Code should take appropriate action. Judges having knowledge* that another judge has committed a violation of this Code that raises a substantial question as to the other judge's fitness for office shall inform the appropriate authority.*

(2) Judges who receive information indicating a substantial likelihood that a lawyer has committed a violation of the Standards of Conduct of the State Bar of Georgia should take appropriate action. Judges having knowledge* that a lawyer has committed a violation of the Standards of Conduct of the State Bar of Georgia that raises a substantial question as to the lawyer's honesty, trustworthiness, or fitness as a lawyer in other respects shall inform the appropriate authority.*

(3) Acts of judges, in the discharge of disciplinary responsibilities, required or permitted by Sections 3D(1) and 3D(2) are part of their judicial duties and shall be absolutely privileged, and no civil action predicated thereon may be instituted against these judges.

Commentary: Appropriate action may include direct communication with the judge or lawyer who has committed the violation, or other direct action if available, and reporting the violation to the appropriate authority or other agency or body. Section 3D(1) requires judges to inform the Judicial Qualifications Commission of any other judge's violation of the Code of Judicial Conduct, if the violation raises a substantial question of fitness for office and if the violation is actually known to the reporting judge. Section 3D(2) also requires judges to report to the State Bar of Georgia any violation by a lawyer of the Standards of Conduct, if the violation raises a substantial question of the lawyer's fitness as a lawyer and, again, if the violation is actually known to the reporting judge.

E. Disqualification

(1) Judges shall disqualify themselves in any proceeding in which their impartiality might reasonably be questioned, including but not limited to instances where:

Commentary: Under this rule, judges are subject to disqualification whenever their impartiality might reasonably be questioned, regardless of whether any of the specific rules in Section 3E(1) apply. For example, if a judge were in the process of negotiating for employment with a law firm, the judge would be disqualified from any matters in which that firm appeared, unless the disqualification was waived by the parties after disclosure by the judge. Judges should disclose on the record information that the court believes the parties or their lawyers might consider relevant to the question of disqualification, even if they believe there is no legal basis for disqualification. The rule of necessity may override the rule of disqualification. For example, a judge might he required to participate in judicial review of a judicial salary statute, or might be the only judge available in a matter requiring immediate judicial action, such as a hearing on probable cause or a temporary restraining order. In the latter case, the judge must disclose on the record the basis for possible disqualification and use reasonable efforts to transfer the matter to another judge as soon as possible.

    (a) the judge has a personal bias or prejudice concerning a party or a party's lawyer, or personal knowledge* of disputed evidentiary facts concerning the proceeding;

    (b) the judge served as a lawyer in the matter of controversy, or a lawyer with whom the judge previously practiced law served during such association as a lawyer concerning the matter, or the judge has been a material witness concerning it;

Commentary: A lawyer in a government agency does not ordinarily have an association with other lawyers employed by that agency within the meaning of Section 3E(1)(b); judges formerly employed by a governmental agency, however, should disqualify themselves in a proceeding if their impartiality might reasonably be questioned because of such association.

    (c) the judge or the judge's spouse, or a person within the third degree of relationship* to either of them, or the spouse of such a person, or any other member of the judge's family residing in the judge's household*:

        (i) is a party to the proceeding, or an officer, director, or trustee of a party;

        (ii) is acting as a lawyer in the proceeding;

        (iii) is known* by the judge to have a more than de minimis* interest that could be substantially affected by the proceeding;

        (iv) is to the judge's knowledge* likely to be a material witness in the proceeding.

Commentary: The fact that a lawyer in a proceeding is affiliated with a law firm with which a relative of the judge is affiliated does not of itself disqualify the judge. Under appropriate circumstances, the fact that "the judge's impartiality might reasonably be questioned" under Section 3E(1), or that the relative is known by the judge to have an interest in the law firm that could be "substantially affected by the outcome of the proceeding" under Section 3E(1)(c)(iii) requires the judge's disqualification.

    (2) Judges shall keep informed about their personal and fiduciary* economic interests,* and make a reasonable effort to keep informed about the personal financial interests of their spouses and minor children residing in their households.

F. Remittal of Disqualification.

    Judges disqualified by the terms of Section 3E may disclose on the record the basis of their disqualification and may ask the parties and their lawyers to consider, out of the presence of the judge, whether to waive disqualification. If following disclosure of any basis for disqualification other than personal bias or prejudice concerning a party, the parties and lawyers, without participation by the judge, all agree that the judge should not be

disqualified, and the judge is then willing to participate, the judge may participate in the proceeding. The agreement shall be incorporated in the record of the proceeding.

Commentary: A remittal procedure provides the parties an opportunity to proceed without delay if they wish to waive the disqualification. To ensure that consideration of the question of remittal is made independently to the court, judges must not solicit, seek or hear comment on possible remittal or waiver of the disqualification, unless the lawyers jointly propose remittal after consultation as provided in Section 3F. A party may act through counsel, if counsel represents on the record that the party has been consulted and consents. As a practical matter, judges may wish to have all parties and their lawyers sign a remittal agreement.

Canon 4

Judges May Engage in Activities to Improve the Law, the Legal System, and the Administration of Justice.

Judges, subject to the proper performance of their judicial duties, may not engage in the following quasi-judicial activities, if in so doing they cast doubt on their capacity to decide impartially any issue that may come before them;

A. Judges may speak, write, lecture, teach, and participate in other activities concerning the law,* the legal system, and the administration of justice.

B. Judges may appear at public hearings before an executive or legislative body or official on matters concerning the law,* the legal system, and the administration of justice, and they may otherwise consult with an executive or legislative body or official, but only on matters concerning the administration of justice.

C. Judges may serve as members, officers, or directors of an organization or governmental agency devoted to the improvement of the law,* the legal system, or the administration of justice. They may assist such organizations in raising funds and may participate in their management and investment, but should not personally participate in public fund raising activities. They may make recommendations to public and private fund-granting agencies on projects and programs concerning the law, the legal system, and the administration of justice.

Commentary: As a judicial officer and person specially learned in the law, a judge is in a unique position to contribute to the improvement of the law, the legal system, and the administration of justice, including revision of substantive and procedural law and improvement of criminal and juvenile justice. To the extent that time permits, judges are encouraged to do so, either independently or through a bar association, judicial conference, or other organization dedicated to the improvement of the law. Non-quasi-judicial, or non-law-related, extra-judicial activities are governed by Canon 5.

Canon 5

Judges Shall Regulate Their Extra-Judicial Activities to Minimize the Risk of Conflict with Their Judicial Duties.

A. Avocational Activities.

Judges may not engage in such avocational activities as detract from the dignity of their office or interfere with the performance of their judicial duties.

Commentary: Complete separation of judges from extra-judicial activities is neither possible nor wise; they should not become isolated from the society in which they live.

B. Civic and Charitable Activities.

Judges may not participate in civic and charitable activities that reflect adversely upon their impartiality or interfere with the performance of their judicial duties. Judges may serve as officers, directors, trustees, or non-legal advisors of educational, religious, charitable, fraternal, or civic organizations not conducted for the economic or political advantage of their members, subject to the following limitations:

(1) Judges shall not serve if it is likely that the organization will be engaged in proceedings that would ordinarily come before them or will be regularly engaged in adversary proceedings in any court.

Commentary: The changing nature of some organizations and of their relationship to the law makes it necessary for judges regularly to reexamine the activities of each organization with which they are affiliated to determine whether it is proper for them to continue their relationship with it. For example, in many jurisdictions charitable hospitals are now more frequently in court than in the past. Similarly, the boards of some legal aid organizations now make policy decisions that may have political significance or imply commitment to causes that may come before the courts for adjudication.

(2) Judges shall not solicit funds for any educational, religious, charitable, fraternal, or civic organization, or use or permit the use of the prestige of their office for that purpose, but they may be listed as officers, directors, or trustees of such organizations. A judge should not be a speaker or the guest of honor at any organization's fund raising event, but may attend such events.

(3) Judges shall not give investment advice to such an organization, but they may serve on its board of directors or trustees even though it has the responsibility for approving investment decisions.

Commentary: A judge's participation in an organization devoted to quasi-judicial, or law-related, extra-judicial activities is governed by Canon 4.

C. Financial Activities.

(1) Judges should refrain from financial and business dealings with lawyers, litigants, and others that tend to reflect adversely on their impartiality, interfere with the proper performance of their judicial duties, or exploit their judicial positions.

(2) Subject to the requirement of subsection (1), judges may hold and manage investments, including real estate, and engage in other remunerative activity including the operation of a business.

(3) Judges should manage their investments and other financial interests to minimize the number of cases in which they are disqualified. As soon as they can do so without serious financial detriment they should divest themselves of investments and other financial interests that might require frequent disqualification.

(4) Neither judges nor members of their families residing in their households* should accept a substantial gift, bequest, favor, or loan from anyone except as follows:

(a) judges may accept gifts incident to a public testimonial to them; books supplied by publishers on a complimentary basis for official use; or invitations to judges and their spouses to attend bar-related functions or activities devoted to the improvement of the law,* the legal system, or the administration of justice;

(b) judges or members of their families residing in their households may accept ordinary social hospitality; a gift, bequest, favor, or loan from a relative; a wedding or engagement gift; a loan from a lending institution in its regular course of business on the same terms generally available to persons who are not judges, or a scholarship or fellowship awarded on the same terms applied to other applicants.

(c) judges or members of their families residing in their households may accept any other gift, bequest, favor, or loan only if the donor is not a party or other person whose interests have come or are likely to come before them, and if its value exceeds $100, the judges report it in the same manner as they report compensation in Canon 6C.

Commentary: This subsection does not apply to contributions to a judge's campaign for judicial office, a matter governed by Canon 7.

(5) Judges are not required by this Code to disclose their income, debts, or investments, except as provided in this Canon and Canons 3 and 6.

Commentary: Canon 3 requires judges to disqualify themselves in any proceeding in which they have a financial interest; Canon 5 requires judges to refrain from financial activities that might interfere with the impartial performance of their judicial duties; Canon 6 requires them to report all compensation they receive for activities involving personal services outside their judicial office. Judges have the rights of an ordinary citizen, including the right to privacy in their financial affairs, except to the extent that limitations thereon are required to safeguard the proper performance of their duties. Owning and receiving income from investments do not as such affect the performance of a judge's duties.

(6) Information acquired by judges in their judicial capacity should not be used or disclosed by them in financial dealings or for any purpose not related to their judicial duties.

D. Fiduciary* Activities.

Judges should not serve as executors, administrators, trustees, guardians, or other fiduciaries, except for the estates, trusts, or persons of members of their families and then only if such service will not interfere with the proper performance of their judicial duties. "Members of their families" include a spouse, child, grandchild, parent, grandparent, or other relative or person with whom the judge maintains a close familial relationship. As family fiduciaries, judges are subject to the following restrictions:

(1) They should not serve if it is likely that as fiduciaries, they will be engaged in proceedings that would ordinarily come before them, or if the estates, trusts, or wards become involved in adversary proceedings in the court on which they serve or one under its appellate jurisdiction.

(2) While acting as fiduciaries, judges are subject to the same restrictions on financial activities that apply to them in their personal capacities.

Commentary: Judges' obligations under this Canon and their obligations as fiduciaries may come into conflict. For example, a judge should resign as trustee if it would result in detriment to the trust to divest it of holdings whose retention would place the judge in violation of Canon 5C(3).

E. Arbitration.

Judges shall not act as arbitrators or mediators for compensation. This prohibition does not apply to senior judges who serve as judges.

F. Practice of Law.

Judges shall not practice law, unless allowed by law.*

G Extra-Judicial Appointments.

A judge should not accept appointment to a governmental committee, commission, or other position that is concerned with issues of fact or policy on matters other than the improvement of the law,* the legal system, or the administration of justice, if acceptance of such appointment might reasonably cast doubt upon the judge's impartiality or demean the judge's office.

Commentary: Valuable services have been rendered in the past to the states and the nation by judges appointed by the executive to undertake important extra-judicial assignments. The appropriateness of conferring these assignments on judges must be reassessed, however, in light of the demands on judicial manpower created by today's crowded dockets and the need to protect the courts from involvement in extra-judicial matters that may prove to be controversial. Judges should not be expected or permitted to accept governmental appointments that could interfere with the effectiveness and independence of the judiciary.

Canon 6

Judges Should Regularly File Reports of Compensation Received for Quasi-Judicial and Extra-Judicial Related Activities.

Judges may not receive compensation and reimbursement of expenses for the quasi-judicial and extra-judicial activities permitted by this Code, if the source of such payments gives the appearance of influencing the judge in his judicial duties or otherwise gives the appearance of impropriety. Such compensation is subject to the following restrictions:

A. Compensation.

Compensation should not exceed a reasonable amount nor should it exceed what a person who is not a judge would receive for the same activity.

B. Expense Reimbursement.

Expense reimbursement should be limited to the actual cost of travel, food, lodging, and other necessary expense reasonably incurred by the judge and, where appropriate to the occasion, by the judge's spouse. Any payment in excess of such an amount is compensation.

C. Reports.

Except as hereinafter provided to the contrary, full-time judges should report the dates, places, and nature of any activities involving personal services for which they received compensation, and the name of the payor and the amount of compensation so received. Compensation or income of a spouse attributed to the judge by operation of a community property law is not extra-judicial compensation to the judge. Judges' reports for each calendar year should be filed between January first and April fifteenth of the following year in the office of the Clerk of the Supreme Court of Georgia. A copy of a judge's federal income tax return shall be considered a sufficient compliance with this paragraph. Such report or tax return shall be filed under seal and shall be available for inspection only by the Justices of the Supreme Court of Georgia and the members of the Judicial Qualifications Commission.

∞ Canon 7

Judges Shall Refrain from Political Activity Inappropriate to Their Judicial Office.

A. Political Conduct in General.

   (1) A judge or a candidate* for public election* to judicial office shall not:
       (a) act or hold himself or herself out as a leader or hold any office in a political organization*;
       (b) make speeches for a political organization or candidate or publicly endorse a candidate for public office;

Commentary: A candidate does not publicly endorse another candidate for public office by having his name on the same ticket.

       (c) solicit funds for or pay an assessment or make a contribution to a political organization, or purchase tickets for political party dinners, or other functions, except as authorized in subsection A(2).
   (2) Judges holding an office filled by public election* between competing candidates,* or candidates for such office, may attend political gatherings and speak to such gatherings on their own behalf when they are candidates for election or re-election.

B. Campaign Conduct

   (1) Candidates,* including an incumbent judge, for any judicial office that is filled by public election* between competing candidates:
       (a) shall prohibit officials or employees subject to their direction or control from doing for them what they are prohibited from doing under this Canon and shall not allow any other person to do for them what they are prohibited from doing under this Canon;
       (b) shall not make statements that commit the candidate with respect to issues likely to come before the court;

Commentary: This Canon does not prohibit a judge or a candidate from publicly stating his or her personal views on disputed issues, see Republican Party V. White, 536 U.S. 765 (2002). To ensure that voters understand a judge's duty to uphold the constitution and laws of Georgia where the law differs from his or her personal belief, however, judges and candidates are encouraged to emphasize in any public statement their duty to uphold the law regardless of their personal views.

       (c) shall not use or participate in the publication of a false statement of fact concerning themselves or their candidacies, or concerning any opposing candidate or candidacy, with knowledge of the statement's falsity or with reckless disregard for the statement's truth or falsity;

Commentary: The determination of whether a candidate knows of falsity or recklessly disregards the truth or falsity of his or her public communication is an objective one, from the viewpoint of a "reasonable attorney," using the standard of "objective malice." See In re Chmura, 608 N.W. 2d 31 (Mich. 2000)

(d) shall be responsible for the content of any statement or advertisement published or communicated in any medium by a campaign committee if the candidate knew of or recklessly disregarded the content of said statement or advertisement prior to its release;

(e) and except where a statement or advertisement is published or communicated by a third party, shall be responsible for reviewing and approving the content of his or her statements and advertisements, and those of his or her campaign committee. Failure to do so will not be a defense to a complaint for violation of this Canon.

(2) Candidates,* including an incumbent judge, for a judicial office that is filled by public election* between competing candidates, may personally solicit campaign contributions and publicly stated support. Candidates, including incumbent judges, should not use or permit the use of campaign contributions for the private benefit of themselves or members of their families.

Commentary: Although judges and judicial candidates are free to personally solicit campaign contributions and publicly stated support, see Weaver Bonner, 309 F 3d 1312 (11th Cir. 2002), they are encouraged to establish campaign committees of responsible persons to secure and manage the expenditure of funds for their campaigns and to obtain public statements of support of their candidacies. The use of campaign committees is encouraged because they may better maintain campaign decorum and reduce campaign activity that may cause requests for recusal or the appearance of partisanship with respect to issues or the parties which require recusal.

C. Applicability

(a) This Canon generally applies to all incumbent judges and judicial candidates.* A successful candidate, whether or not an incumbent, is subject to judicial discipline by the Judicial Qualifications Commission for his or her campaign conduct.

(b) A lawyer who is a candidate* for judicial office shall comply with all provisions of the Code of Judicial Conduct applicable to candidates* for judicial office. An unsuccessful lawyer candidate* is subject to discipline for campaign conduct by the State Bar of Georgia pursuant to applicable standards of the State Bar of Georgia, and the Judicial Qualifications Commission shall immediately report any such alleged conduct to the office of the General Counsel of the State Bar of Georgia for such action as may be appropriate under applicable bar rules.

(c) An unsuccessful non-lawyer candidate* is subject to discipline for campaign misconduct by the Judicial Qualifications Commission, and in addition to any other sanctions authorized by the Rules of the Judicial Qualifications Commission, the Commission, after full hearing, is authorized to recommend that such individual be barred from seeking any elective or appointive judicial office in this State for a period not to exceed 10 years.

Application of the Code of Judicial Conduct

Anyone, whether or not a lawyer, who is an officer of a judicial system performing judicial functions, including an officer such as an administrative law judge of an executive branch agency or of the Board of Workers Compensation, an associate judge, special master, or magistrate, or any person who is a candidate for any such office is a judge for the purpose of this Code. All judges shall comply with this Code except as provided below.

A. Part-time judges.

A part-time judge is a judge who serves on a continuing or periodic basis, but is permitted by law to devote time to some other profession or occupation and whose compensation for that reason is less than that of a full-time judge. Part-time judges:

(1) are not required to comply with Canon 5D [fiduciary activities], 5E [arbitration], 5F [practice of law], and 5G [extra-judicial appointments], and are not required to comply with Canon 6C [annual financial reporting].

(2) should not practice law in the court on which they serve, or in any court subject to the appellate jurisdiction of the court on which they serve, or act as lawyers in proceedings in which they have served as judges or in any proceeding related thereto.

B. Judge Pro Tempore.

A judge pro tempore is a person who is appointed to act temporarily as a judge.

(1) While acting as such, a judge pro tempore is not required to comply with Canon 5C(3) [financial activities], 5D [fiduciary activities], 5E [arbitration and mediation], 5F [practice of law], and 5G [extra-judicial appointments], and Canon 6C [annual financial reporting].

2) Persons who have been judges pro tempore should not act as lawyers in proceedings in which they have served as judges or in other proceeding related thereto.

C. Time for Compliance.

A person to whom this Code becomes applicable shall comply immediately with all provisions of this Code except Sections 5C(1), 5C(2), 5C(3) [personal and family financial activities] and 5D [fiduciary activities], and shall comply with these Sections as soon as reasonably possible and shall do so in any event within the period of one year.

Commentary: If serving as a fiduciary when selected as judge, a new judge may, notwithstanding the prohibitions in Section 5D, continue to serve, but only for that period of time necessary to avoid serious adverse consequences to the beneficiary of the fiduciary relationship, and in no event longer than 1 year. Similarly, if engaged at the time of judicial selection in a business activity, a new judge may, notwithstanding the prohibitions in Section 5C(1), 5C(2), and 5C(3), continue in that activity for a reasonable period, but in no event longer than 1 year.

D. In addition to the foregoing, the Commission shall have continuing jurisdiction over individuals to whom this Code is applicable regarding allegations of misconduct occurring during such individual's service as an officer of a judicial system if a complaint is filed no later than one (1) year following service of such judicial officer.

This Code shall become effective January 7, 2004.

Like lawyers, accountants are also bound to a code of professional conduct. The American Institute of Certified Public Accountants authorizes this code, which you may find in its entirety at http://www. aicpa.org/RESEARCH/STANDARDS/CODEOFCONDUCT/Pages/ default.aspx

The Code of Professional Conduct of the American Institute of Certified Public Accountants is divided into seven sections. The first section, Principles, provides the framework for the remaining sections, which govern the performance of professional services by members. The code provides guidance and rules to all members—those in public practice, in industry, in government, and in education—in the performance of their professional responsibilities. Compliance, as with all standards in an open society, depends primarily on members' understanding and voluntary actions, secondarily on reinforcement by peers and public opinion, and ultimately on disciplinary proceedings, when necessary, against members who fail to comply with the Code.

The Principles of the code are in Section 50 and consist of the Preamble and the six articles that follow.

Article I—Responsibilities

In carrying out their responsibilities as professionals, members should exercise sensitive professional and moral judgments in all their activities.

Article II—The Public Interest

Members should accept the obligation to act in a way that will serve the public interest, honor the public trust, and demonstrate commitment to professionalism.

Article III—Integrity

To maintain and broaden public confidence, members should perform all professional responsibilities with the highest sense of integrity.

Article IV—Objectivity and Independence

A member should maintain objectivity and be free of conflicts of interest in discharging professional responsibilities. A member in public practice should be independent in fact and appearance when providing auditing and other attestation services.

Article V—Due Care

A member should observe the profession's technical and ethical standards, strive continually to improve competence and the quality of services, and discharge professional responsibility to the best of the member's ability.

Article VI—Scope and Nature of Services

A member in public practice should observe the Principles of the Code of Professional Conduct in determining the scope and nature of services to be provided.

REFERENCE: (2008). Code of professional conduct and bylaws. Ewing, NJ: American Institute of Certified Public Accountants.

A Certified Public Accountant (CPA) license is issued to individuals that have met the education, experience and examination requirements. The Uniform CPA Examination is the exam required for licensure as Certified Public Accountant in any of the fifty-five U.S. jurisdictions (the fifty states, the District of Columbia, Puerto Rico, the U. S. Virgin Islands, Guam and the Commonwealth of Northern Mariana Islands). According to the exam's mission statement, its purpose is "To admit individuals into the accounting profession only after they have demonstrated the entry-level knowledge and skills necessary to protect the public interest in a rapidly changing business and financial environment." The American Institute of Certified Public Accountants Board of Examiners approves content and skill specifications for the Uniform CPA Examination.

The CPA Exam consists of four sections: Auditing and Attestation (AUD), Business Environment and Concepts (BEC), Financial Accounting and Reporting (FAR) and Regulation (REG). The content areas associated with each section follow, along with the percentage of questions on the exam.

Auditing and Attestation

Covers knowledge of auditing procedures, generally accepted auditing standards and other standards related to attest engagements, as well as the skills needed to apply that knowledge. It consists of:

    I. Auditing and Attestation: Engagement Acceptance and Understanding the Assignment (12–16%).

    II. Auditing and Attestation: Understanding the Entity and its Environment (Including Internal Control) (16–20%).

    III. Auditing and Attestation: Performing Audit Procedures and Evaluations Evidence (16–20%).

    IV. Auditing and Attestation: Evaluation Audit Findings, Communications, and Reporting (16–20%).

    V. Accounting and Review Services Engagements (12–16%).

    VI. Professional Responsibilities (15–20%).

Business Environment and Concepts (BEC)

Covers knowledge of the general business environment and business concepts that candidates need to know in order to understand the underlying business reasons for and the accounting implications of business transactions, along with the skills needed to apply that knowledge. The content areas include:

I. Corporate Governance (16–20%)
II. Economic Concepts and Analysis (16–20%)
III. Financial Management (19–23%)
IV. Information Systems and Communication (15–19%)
V. Strategic Planning (10–14%)
VI. Operations Management (12–16%)

Financial Accounting and Reporting (FAR)

Covers knowledge of generally accepted accounting principles for business enterprises, not-for-profit organizations and governmental entities and the skills needed to apply that knowledge. The content areas are:

I. Conceptual Framework, Standards, Standard Setting and Presentation of Financial Statements (17–20%)
II. Financial Statement Accounts: Recognition, Measurement, Valuation, Calculation, Presentation and Disclosures (27–33%)
III. Specific Transactions, Events and Disclosures: Recognition, Measurement, Valuation, Calculation, Presentation and Disclosures (27–33%)
IV. Government Accounting and Reporting (8–12%)
V. Not-for-Profit (Nongovernmental)Accounting and Reporting (8%–12%)

Regulation (REG)

Covers knowledge of federal taxation, ethics, professional and legal responsibilities, and business law, and the skills needed to apply that knowledge. Included are:

I. Ethics, Professional and Legal Responsibilities (15–19%)
II. Business Law (17–21%)
III. Federal Tax Process, Procedures, Accounting, and Planning (11–15%)
IV. Federal Taxation of Property Transactions (12–16%)
V. Federal Taxation of Entities (18–24%)

An individual's skill is measured in the categories of knowledge and understanding, application of the body of knowledge and written communication. During the exam, individuals have access to a calculator, authoritative literature, spreadsheets or database tools. Multiple-choice questions measure knowledge and understanding. The percentage of multiple choice questions in the FAR, REG and AUD sections is 50 to 60%; the BEC contains 80 to 90%. Task-based simulations measure the application of the body of knowledge and account for 40 to 50% of the FAR, REG and AUD questions. Finally, the essay responses assess the written communication, amounting to 10 to 20% of the questions in the BEC section.

REFERENCE: Board of Examiners (2008). Content and skill specifications for the uniform CPA examination. Ewing, NJ., American Institute of Certified Public Accountants.

The Multistate Bar Examination (MBE)

∞ Description of the MBE

The Multistate Bar Examination is an objective six-hour examination containing 200 questions. The examination is divided into two periods of three hours each, one in the morning and one in the afternoon, with 100 questions in each period. The examination includes 190 live test questions in the following areas: Constitutional Law, Contracts, Criminal Law and Procedure, Evidence, Real Property, and Torts. There are 33 questions each in Contracts and Torts and 31 questions each in Constitutional Law, Criminal Law and Procedure, Evidence, and Real Property. In addition, the exam contains 10 pretest questions that are indistinguishable from the live test items, but will not be used for scoring purposes.

The questions on the examination are designed to be answered by applying fundamental legal principles rather than local case or statutory law. A given question may indicate the applicable statute, theory of liability, or comparable principle of law.

Many of the questions require applicants to analyze the legal relationships arising from a fact situation or to take a position as an advocate. Some questions call for suggestions about interpreting, drafting, or counseling that might lead to more effective structuring of a transaction.

All questions are multiple choice. Applicants are asked to choose the best answer from the four stated alternatives. The test is designed to give credit only when the applicant has selected the best answer. Therefore, applicants should mark only one answer for each question; multiple answers will not be counted.

Scores are based on the number of questions answered correctly. Applicants are, therefore, advised to answer every question. Time should be used effectively. Applicants should not hurry, but should work steadily and as quickly as possible without sacrificing accuracy. If a question seems too difficult, the applicant is advised to go on to the next one and come back to the skipped question later.

Answer sheets are centrally scored. Both raw scores and scaled scores are computed for each applicant. A raw score is the number of questions answered correctly. Raw scores on different forms of the test are not comparable primarily due to differences in the difficulty of the test forms.

A statistical process called equating adjusts for variations in the difficulty of different forms of the examination so that any particular scaled score will represent the same level of performance from test to test.

For instance, if a test were more difficult than previous tests, then the scaled scores on that test would be adjusted upward to account for this difference. The purpose of these adjustments is to help ensure that no applicant is unfairly penalized (or rewarded) for taking a more (or less) difficult form of the test.

⬭ Myths and Facts about the MBE

Bar Examiners across the country often encounter questions and myths relating to the Multistate Bar Examination (MBE), one of the important parts of their test of minimum competence for licensure to practice law. Over the years, significant research has been conducted that dispels these myths.

Myth 1

Examinees can pass the MBE by guessing. The MBE is a test of memory and test-taking ability, not of legal knowledge or analytical skill.

Fact

Research indicates that the MBE is not a "multiple-guess test" or an examination that rewards test-taking ability. In research conducted in July 1986, incoming law students took the morning session of the MBE, and their scores were compared with graduates of the same law schools who had taken the same examination. The novices and graduates had virtually identical mean LSAT scores, so if the ability to take multiple-choice tests were the major factor influencing MBE scores, both groups should have had very similar MBE scores. In fact, the highest MBE score earned by the novices was lower than the lowest score earned by any of the graduates.

Second, research on the MBE indicates that MBE scores are highly correlated with other measures of legal skills and knowledge, such as scores on state essay examinations and law school grades. These correlations provide empirical evidence that the MBE is testing legal ability rather than general test-taking ability. Similarly, a panel of experts convened in 1992 as part of a content validity study concluded that MBE items were material to the practice of law and that their emphasis was balanced between legal reasoning skills and memorization of legal principles.

Myth 2

MBE questions are needlessly difficult, arcane, and tricky.

Fact

MBE questions are designed to be a fair index of whether an applicant has the ability to practice law. MBE questions are written by drafting committees composed of men and women who are law teachers and practitioners. Before it is administered, every MBE question is reviewed at several levels: at least twice as it is edited by the drafting committee; by psychometric experts to insure that it is fair and unbiased; by the practitioner members of the MBE Policy Committee and their academic consultants; and by the members of boards of bar examiners across the country. After a form of the MBE is administered, any question that performs in an unanticipated manner—is very difficult or is missed by applicants who did well on the rest of the test—is flagged by psychometric experts and reviewed again by content experts on the drafting committees to ensure that no ambiguity exists in the question and that the key is unequivocally correct. Should an error be detected even after this thorough scrutiny, two or more answers may be deemed correct in order to ensure that no applicant is disadvantaged by having a particular question appear on the form of the MBE he or she took.

In a 1992 study, expert panelists reported that they believed MBE items were generally easy, correctly estimating that about 66 percent of candidates would select the right answer to a typical item. A study is underway to review the MBE test specifications (subject matter outlines) in order to make certain that the questions asked on the examination continue to relate to knowledge that is important to the practice of law.

Myth 3

Not enough time is allotted to answer MBE questions.

Fact

Research shows that the time allotted to take the MBE is sufficient for 99 percent of applicants. The MBE is designed to be answered by a reasonably competent applicant in the amount of time available. The rate of correct responses at the end of three-hour sessions is not significantly different from the rate of correct answers at other, earlier points in the test.

A research project in which applicants were given virtually unlimited time to answer the MBE resulted in an average increase in score of about 6 raw (unscaled) points. Since all groups benefit from an increase in time to the same degree, and since the test is scaled to account for differences in difficulty, an increase in average score would be offset in the scaling process and additional time would not increase applicants' scaled scores.

Myth 4

Essay examinations and performance tests are a better way to measure minimum competency to practice law.

Fact

While essay examinations and performance tests provide important information about candidates, there are several significant advantages to including multiple-choice tests on a bar examination. First, multiple-choice testing offers the opportunity for a breadth of coverage of subject areas that cannot be duplicated using only essay questions or performance tests. This breadth of coverage improves the reliability of the examination. Second, multiple-choice questions can be scored objectively, and scores can be scaled to adjust for changes in difficulty from one test to the next. There are two sources of variation in difficulty in essay examinations and performance tests: variations in the difficulty of the test items themselves, and variations in how strict or lenient graders are. In contrast, scores on the MBE are equated through a process that ensures that a new form of the MBE is no more nor less difficult than a previous form. By comparing the performance of applicants on a common set of items, raw scores on the test can be converted to adjusted, "scaled" scores that are directly comparable to one another. Because scores are equated, the MBE provides an anchor for other, more subjective test scores; the National Conference recommends that scores on essay examinations and performance tests be scaled to the MBE. And finally, this scaling of MBE scores allows direct comparisons of performance to be made among tests. An applicant taking a current examination is on a level playing field with other applicants taking tests at other times.

Myth 5

The MBE discriminates against minority applicants.

Fact

The MBE neither widens nor narrows the gap in performance level between minority and majority applicants. Research indicates that differences in mean scores among racial and ethnic groups correspond closely to differences in those groups' mean LSAT scores, law school grade-point averages, and scores on other measures of ability to practice law, such as bar examination essay scores or performance test scores. Individual items on the MBE that are relatively difficult for one group are relatively difficult for all groups; the relative difficulty of the items within a subtest (e.g., the Constitutional Law items versus the Torts items) does not differ from group to group. Finally, total MBE scores are not higher or lower from group to group than they are on other test formats.

All items on the MBE are reviewed for potential bias. Men and women serve on each drafting committee, and members of ethnic minority groups assist in the preparation and review of items at both the drafting committee level and at the level of MBE Committee and state Board review. The National Conference of Bar Examiners is committed to diverse representation on all its drafting and policy committees.

Myth 6

The MBE is getting easier; scores keep increasing while applicants are getting less able.

Fact

The MBE is a reliable measure of applicant ability. The average scaled score on the MBE has varied by less than 2 points from year to year, indicating that the ability level of the candidate pool has been fairly stable. Changes in MBE scores follow closely the variations in average scores on other measures of candidate ability, such as the LSAT. This correlation between changes in MBE and LSAT scores indicates that increases in the average score mirror increases in the general ability level of the group being tested rather than a decline in the difficulty of the test.

Jurisdictions Using the MBE in 2013

Alabama	Maine	Oregon
Alaska	Maryland	Pennsylvania
Arizona	Massachusetts	Rhode Island
Arkansas	Michigan	South Carolina
California	Minnesota	South Dakota
Colorado	Mississippi	Tennessee
Connecticut	Missouri	Texas
Delaware	Montana	Utah
District of Columbia	Nebraska	Vermont
Florida	Nevada	Virginia
Georgia	New Hampshire	Washington
Hawaii	New Jersey	West Virginia
Idaho	New Mexico	Wisconsin
Illinois	New York	Wyoming
Indiana	North Carolina	Guam
Iowa	North Dakota	Northern Mariana Is.
Kansas	Ohio	Republic of Palau
Kentucky	Oklahoma	Virgin Islands

Georgia Rules of Professional Conduct EXERCISE

Point value is at the Instructor's discretion

Please provide a complete answer below each question.

❖ **GO TO THIS SITE TO FIND YOUR ANSWERS**

www.gabar.org/barrules/ethics and professionalism/index.cfm

1. What types of rules are the Georgia Rules of Professional Conduct?

2. Should a lawyer abide by the client's decisions in all matters of representation?

3. What client information should a lawyer keep confidential and what is the maximum penalty for violating this rule?

4. Under what circumstances should a lawyer terminate his representation of a client?

5. What does it mean for a lawyer to act as an advisor?

6. How shall a lawyer act to opposing counsel and his or her party in court? What is the maximum penalty for violating this rule?

7. Can a lawyer act as both advocate and witness in the same trial?

8. Should a lawyer communicate with another party whom the lawyer knows is represented by counsel?

9. What are the duties of a partner in a law firm?

10. How many hours of voluntary service should a lawyer aspire to during a calendar year?

Please provide a complete answer using the Georgia Code of Judicial Conduct found in this handbook.

11. What is the definition of invidious discrimination?

12. According to Canon _____, judges should act in what way to uphold the integrity and independence of the judiciary?

13. Can judges voluntarily testify as witnesses at trials?

14. Does a judge have any administrative responsibilities? If so, what are they?

15. Are judges allowed to assist organizations in raising funds?

16. Should judges participate in financial dealings with lawyers?

17. Can a judge's family members, who reside in the judge's household, receive substantial gifts?

18. Expense reimbursement should be limited to the _____ of travel, food, lodging, and other necessary expense _____ incurred by the judge and, where _____ to the occasion, by the judge's spouse. Any payment in excess of such an amount is compensation.

19. What limitations does a judge have as a candidate for public office?

20. What is the definition of a judge pro tempore?

Please provide a complete answer using the American Institute of Certified Public Accountants Code of Proffesional Conduct fount at

http://www.aicpa.org/RESEARCH/STANDARDS/CODEOFCONDUCT/Pages/default.aspx.

21. By becoming a member of the AICPA, an accountant assumes what type of obligation?

22. According to Section #_____, how is integrity measured?

23. What is the definition of a "joint closely held investment"?

24. Would objectivity or integrity be considered to be impaired if a member offers or accepts gifts or entertainment to or from a client or a customer or vendor of the member's employer?

25. Which rule states, "that a member shall not state affirmatively that financial statements or other financial data of an entity are presented in conformity with generally accepted accounting principles (GAAP) if such statements or data contain any departure from an accounting principle promulgated by a body designated by Council to establish such principles that has a material effect on the statements or data taken as a whole"?

26. Can a member disclose any confidential client information?

27. May a member in public practice disclose the name of a client for whom the member or the member's firm performed professional services?

28. Is failing to file personal taxes a discredit to the accounting profession?

29. Are referral fees allowed?

30. Are members ethically responsible for the acts of their non-certified public accountant partners?

Point value is at the Instructor's discretion

Pleas explain and give complete answers to all questions in order to receive full credit.

31. What are the six subjects of law covered in this *Business, Law, and Ethics Handbook*?

32. List and explain Nash's, Drucker's, Buffet's, Blanchard's and Peale's comprehensive approach for resolving ethical dilemmas.

33. What is one of the key features and main components for understanding law?

34. What is *legal reasoning*?

35. What shapes, at least to some extent, the process of legal reasoning?

36. What are the four basic steps in the legal reasoning process? Please state and explain each step.

37. What questions should you ask to apply the IRAC method?

38. Critical thinking skills are crucial in law. Therefore, when discussing an emotional legal topic, always remember the issue and process your thoughts. Please provide thirteen tips that will help you stay focused on the issue.

39. What are the four focus areas of contract law?

40. What is the most important area of contract law?

41. There are four focus points that students should always underline when answering a contract question. What are those points?

42. Constitutional law is divided into four broad categories. Please list them.

43. In order to convict one of a crime two elements must exist and concur. What are those two elements? Explain fully with complete details.

44. There are two areas of constitutional law students must know well in order to be successful on a constitutional law test. What are those two areas?

45. What are the areas under individual rights that are most heavily tested?

46. The law of evidence is _____. *Explain fully.*

47. What are the four areas of evidence law that must receive special attention and that one must fully understand?

48. What is the trickiest area for most people when learning evidence law?

49. What must you underline in order to understand the fact pattern in a real property question?

50. What are the five key areas of property law that define the type of property? Please explain each.

51. Please list the five broad categories of tort law and tort liability.

52. What is the starting point in the analysis of torts questions?

53. Students should note and think through the _____ before evaluating the possible answers to a question.

54. In a negligence, case there will always be a question of _____.

55. Please answer completely and in accordance with your handbook. What are the key differences between civil law and criminal law?

Answers to Questions

Constitutional Law

Question 1

D. The Supremacy Clause says that any state law that conflicts with a federal law will be struck down. The state policy conflicts with the federal law by basing voting rights solely on citizenship.

Question 2

A. The Equal Protection Clause is raised when a law limits the liberties of some people, but not all people. Kansas's law applies only to motorcyclists, not other motorists.

Question 3

C. Rational basis applies to the Kansas law because the issue at hand is a social welfare issue, similar to seat belt laws. The law does not cover race, national origin, gender, or legitimacy issues.

Question 4

A. The test for rational basis is whether or not the law in question has any rational basis that relates to a legitimate government interest.

Question 5

B. Applying the test for rational basis scrutiny, requiring the use of helmets on a vehicle which totally exposes a rider to outside elements is a rational request that is related to the government interest of keeping motorists safe from harm. This interest can be categorized as legitimate under the state's right to issue laws for the public health and safety of those who use the state's facilities.

Question 6

B. The Commerce Clause allows the U.S. Congress to regulate all things that affect interstate commerce. If Congress can show that bicycles being stolen in one state, then kept or resold in another state affects interstate commerce, then this law would be constitutional.

Question 7

D. The First Amendment protects political speech, which allows a person to vote for or support or oppose candidates for election, proposed laws, or other political issues. Limiting the amount of money a person can give to support or use to oppose political issues reduces or restricts expression of speech in the political area.

Question 8

A. The separation of powers provision of the Constitution gives the power to tax and spend to the United States Congress.

Question 9

B. Although each adult person's tax is calculated based on his or her individual height and weight, every adult person is being taxed. The effect of the tax may differ based on the height and weight calculations, but the tax is uniformly applied to all adult persons.

Question 10

D. Standing dictates that in order to file a lawsuit, a person must have a stake in the controversy at issue, and must stand to gain or lose something without being able to file a lawsuit on that issue. Unless we know that the horse owner will lose the use of state land to walk his or her horse, we don't know whether standing exists for this lawsuit.

Contract Law

Question 1

C. The elements of an offer include serious intent: how serious the offeror was in making the offer; definiteness of terms: does the offer indicate exactly what the contract will be about; and communication: was the offer effectively communicated to the offeree.

Question 2

A. A contract has to have definite terms that the parties can mutually agree upon. Here, Roy's bid didn't include the materials or price points that Shane wanted, and Shane and Roy did not finalize when the performance on the project was to begin. They were still in negotiation when Shane changed his mind.

Question 3

B. Promissory estoppel says that if someone justifiably relies on a promise to his detriment, then justice can be served by making the promisor perform. Roy relied on Shane's discussions of the project and to his detriment spent money by preparing for the job. If Roy can show his reliance was justifiable, which it may not be because there were no finalized plans at the time Roy purchased the superior materials, then Roy can recover under this theory.

Question 4

C. Consideration requires something exchanged that has legal value, not economic value, and is bargained for. The fairness or adequacy of the consideration is not considered here because there is no fraud, duress, or undue influence involved.

Question 5

A. John's neighbor made a clear promise on which John justifiably relied to his detriment; he lost profits on bicycle jobs because he had to assemble the shed himself. Enforcing the neighbor's promise, or the value of it, will serve the best interests of justice.

Question 6

C. Val's Foods doesn't have to perform their contract obligations if Sun Farms fails to meet a state contract condition. The condition here is a condition precedent: if the tomatoes do not pass inspection, Val's Foods is not required to buy them.

Question 7

B. Sun Farms' inability to buy tomatoes at the higher market price meets the requirement of performance becoming too difficult or expensive to be completed. Buying the tomatoes would bankrupt Sun Farms, which is commercial impracticability.

Question 8

D. Sun Farms acted in good faith and delivered as many pesticide-free tomatoes as possible. Their total delivery was only 5 pounds less than the contracted amount to be delivered. A court would likely find that Sun Farms' 995-pound delivery was substantial performance based in good-faith action.

Question 9

C. Both considerations are used to determine the enforceability of liquidated damages clauses. Here, $1 million may be a reasonable estimate of damages because there is a potential for Bruno, other actors, and expensive movie equipment and sets to be damaged. However, if a breach occurred, damages of these things would be easy to establish at the time of the breach. So, this clause would likely not be enforceable.

Question 10

A. To get consequential damages, the breaching party must know in advance of the breach that a breach will cause special damages to the non-breaching party in the form of additional losses. If Xtreme breached the contract knowing that a breach would delay the film's release and result in lost summer movie profits, Bruno may collect consequential damages.

Criminal Law

Question 1

D. Hand was the officer in charge of this and all projects on the railroad line. As officer, he is liable for the acts of his employees and responsible for every detail under the Responsible Corporate Officer Doctrine.

Question 2

A. The backhoe operator is missing the mental state, or mens rea, element of the crime. He was simply doing his job, unaware of the existence of the oil pipeline. Only the officer or supervisor of the project could have known about the oil pipeline, he should have either warned the backhoe operator or taken other precautions to avoid puncturing the pipeline.

Question 3

C. When force or the threat of force is used in the act of theft, the crime is robbery.

Question 4

A. Murder does not require an intent to kill, just to put another's life into unjustifiable risk.

Question 5

A. For murder to work there has to be the mental state, mens rea, and the action, actus reus, of the crime. Here, it was the cancer that killed Gene, not Terry's poisoning attempts, so there is no act of murder present in Gene's death.

Question 6

C. The Constitution prohibits trying the same person twice for the same criminal offense under double jeopardy, but double jeopardy only begins after one trial has rendered a not guilty verdict.

Question 7

D. A waiver of Miranda Rights must be made knowingly and intelligently, meaning that the individual being arrested fully understands what legal rights he or she is giving up.

Question 8

B. Samantha, not knowing that she is receiving stolen goods, is the only non-guilty party in this scenario. Jamie is guilty of theft of the laptop and Phyllis guilty of receiving stolen goods.

Question 9

A. Burglary is defined as unlawful entry into a building with the intent to commit a felony. The actus reus here is the unlawful entry and the mens rea is the intent to commit a felony. Both must be present to find guilt of burglary. Jamie did not have the actus reus of unlawful entry. As an assistant manager of the electronics store, he was given a key to the warehouse, with lawful access at any time.

Question 10

D. Mail fraud and wire fraud occur in Lee and Smith's scheme through the mailing of fraudulent brochures and the fraudulent phone calls to prospective donors. When the donations come into the fake charity, the men pocket that money, committing theft. Finally, Lee bribes his wife to keep quiet, and even though he doesn't have the chance to actually give her the bribe money, a bribe has still been committed merely by offering or soliciting a bribe.

Evidence Law

Question 1

C. Although character evidence is not always allowed, in defamation, character itself is at issue. To prove that Sam harmed her good reputation or character, Lydia has to show what her reputation or character was before Sam's alleged slander. Answer A is hearsay, Answer B is irrelevant, and Answer D is privileged, each of which is normally not admissible evidence.

Question 2

A. In criminal law cases, character evidence is admissible to show character not in keeping with the charged offense. Answer B is hearsay, Answer C is inadmissible in criminal cases, and Answer D is irrelevant, each of which is normally not admissible evidence.

Question 3

B. Although the spousal privilege generally allows spousal communications to remain confidential, an exception to the privilege exists where the spouses have acted jointly to defraud a third party out of something, usually money or a thing of value.

Question 4

C. Impeachment is the process of attempting to harm or destroy a witness's credibility. It is allowable for a party to impeach his or her own witness.

Question 5

D. Hearsay is any statement other than a statement made by the speaker while testifying at the trial and which is offered into evidence in order to prove the truth of the matter asserted. Here, Margot's statement would retell what other speakers had said outside of court and would be used to prove that those speakers committed the crime.

Property Law

Question 1

B. Although the Statute of Frauds does require contracts for the sale of real property to be in writing, when partial performance has begun, that creates an exception to the Statute and allows an oral contract for the sale of real property to be enforced. Both moving into the house and making improvements on it are evidence of partial performance on a home purchase agreement.

Question 2

D. Adverse possession establishes ownership in another's property by the continued use of that property for the statutory time frame, and which use conflicts with the true owner's rights. Here, because Diana was not around to see the use of her property for longer than the specified possession time frame, John takes ownership.

Question 3

C. Tenants in common share ownership in property but have no rights to each other's interest in that property. When Maya and Cameron purchase the home they each gain a half interest in it. Although Cameron tries to convey all the interest in the house to his daughter, he only has legal right to convey what he owns – a half interest. So, Maya retains one half interest and Trisha owns her father's half interest after his death.

Question 4

B. Abandonment serves to extinguish an existing easement when the easement goes unused for a long period of time. Not using a gas pipeline for 20 years could arguably be considered a long period of time.

Question 5

A. Constructive notice is notice that a person exercising ordinary care and diligence would have where actual notice is direct notice. Deliah works as a title examiner in her county, and should easily be aware of how to look up the title of a property to see whether it is still for sale. At the least, she would have ordinary knowledge of how to look up a title to examine whether it is clear or not. If she had completed that diligence, she would have seen that the house she loved was already sold.

Tort Law

Question 1

D. Truth is an absolute defense to a defamation suit, which first and foremost claims that a false statement has been said or written about someone. Second, as mayor, Irene is now a public figure, and public figures have to prove the additional element of malice in defamation claims. Here, malice means that Darla knew that her statement was not true, or recklessly disregarded the truth of the statement but said it anyway. Malice is not present here, again, because Darla's statement is true.

Question 2

C. Conversion is the taking, using, selling, or retaining possession of personal property that belongs to someone else. The taking must occur without the owner knowing about it or having given legal authorization. Here, even though Irene did not take the flowers herself, she authorized the taking and intends to retain them for her products and then sell the flowers as cosmetics.

Question 3

D. Libel per se would offer Darla the easiest case to prove. Saying Darla committed a serious crime (statutory rape) and saying Darla was an unchaste woman are outside the bounds of common decency. A libel per se lawsuit allows Darla to file for guaranteed relief if she can show that the statement is false.

Question 4

B. The assumption of the risk defense states that a Plaintiff who voluntarily enters a risky situation, knowing the risk involved, may not recover for the alleged injury. Traveling at high speeds down an icy and slippery snow-covered hill in a rubber tube poses some risk of injury. As long as the ski resort can prove that Alaina knew the risks involved, they won't have to pay for her injuries. Negligence per se may not work her, if a court decides that the New Hampshire law on skiing does not also apply to snow tubing.

Question 5

A. Comparative negligence allows a negligent plaintiff to recover only for the percentage of her injury that she did not cause herself. Here, if Alaina is somewhat at fault for her own injuries, she could not recover the percentage of fault that is her own. She can only recover the percentage of fault that belongs to the ski resort.

Question 6

C. Stanley is most likely liable for William's injuries because he owned something on his property which enticed a child to enter his property specifically to play with that thing. The court would require Stanley to take precaution and fence in the trampoline or put it away when his grandchildren are not visiting, so that other children are not enticed by it.

Question 7

D. Although this seems like wrongful interference with a contract, an element of that tort is that the third party, who benefits from the breach of contract, knows about the original contract and entices one of the original contracting parties to breach it. Here, Bebsi does not know that Chen already signed a contract with MolaRola; they are just making a job offer.

Question 8

C. The first element of a fraud action is to identify whether there was a misrepresentation of material fact. This misstatement cannot be one of opinion, and puffery, or salesman's talk, is considered puffery under the law. Puffery, the law dictates, cannot be justifiably relied on by a reasonable person, because the salesman is simply trying to "puff up" or improve the look of the item he is trying to sell.

Question 9

B. Although it seems like Roni did not fulfill his duty as tiger caretaker during the party, he is not the owner of the tiger, and would not have intentional tort liability. Mona may be able to show negligence if she can prove that Roni had a duty of care to his party guests to keep them safe.

Question 10

C. Trevor is the owner of the tiger and under strict liability, the owner of wild animals is strictly liable for any injuries the wild animal causes.